ADVANCED NEGOTIATION AND MEDIATION

CONCEPTS, SKILLS, AND EXERCISES

■ ■ ■

By

James R. Holbrook
Clinical Professor of Law
University of Utah

Benjamin J. Cook
Adjunct Professor of Law
Brigham Young University

AMERICAN CASEBOOK SERIES®

WEST®

Mat #41060338

American Casebook Series is a trademark registered in the U.S. Patent and Trademark Office.

© 2013 LEG, Inc. d/b/a West Academic Publishing

    610 Opperman Drive
    St. Paul, MN 55123
    1-800-313-9378

West, West Academic Publishing, and West Academic are trademarks of West Publishing Corporation, used under license.

Printed in the United States of America

ISBN: 978–0–314–26752–8

PREFACE

Basic books on negotiation and mediation are commonplace. Many are well-written and can provide a solid foundation for learning and practice. Less common, and in great need because of the increasing importance of alternative dispute resolution, are books focused on an advanced understanding of mediation and negotiation. This book uniquely incorporates negotiation and mediation concepts and skills into a single volume with the intent to facilitate learning in both theoretical and practical aspects. Accordingly, we incorporate concepts, skills, and exercises into this book to give the reader an opportunity to explore theory, learn skills, and then put the skills into practice.

The book describes four kinds of negotiation and mediation, including performative (for improving communication), transformative (for improving relationships), integrative (for creative problem-solving), and distributive (for a fair exchange of value). We describe a range of skills necessary for effectively creating deals and resolving disputes, summarizing and integrating the salient points of seminal works in the ADR field. We also include a variety of exercises relevant to the topics presented in each chapter.

The Toolbox Approach

Psychologist Abraham Maslow famously wrote that if all you have is a hammer, everything looks like a nail. This caution against over-reliance on one tool is especially appropriate for negotiators and mediators. There is no single right way to negotiate or mediate. Different circumstances require different approaches—a tactic that works well in one context may fail in another. While certain principles may hold true across a number of negotiation or mediation contexts, effective negotiators and mediators are able to read situations and have a variety of approaches they are able to employ. Because of this dynamic nature inherent to negotiation and mediation, it is helpful to think of the various skills and approaches to be used in creating deals or resolving disputes as tools. Increasing the number of process, communication, problem-solving and other tools in their toolbox can help negotiators and mediators to become much more versatile and effective. In addition to using various negotiation and mediation strategies, this book includes a "toolbox" section accompanying each strategy that provides a number of skills that are relevant to the corresponding strategy. The skills can be useful not just for the strategy section in which they are discussed, but in any of the four primary strategies discussed in this book.

Why Negotiation and Mediation in the Same Book?

While negotiation and mediation sit closely at the same end of the dispute resolution spectrum, they may appear to be distinctly different approaches. Negotiation typically involves two or more parties communicating directly, while mediation involves a neutral third party whose role is to help the disputing parties come to an agreement. So why cover both approaches in the same book? We believe that despite procedural differences, negotiation and mediation have much in common conceptually:

- Mediation is often described as facilitated negotiation. Most of the principles, tools, and strategies for effective negotiation are directly applicable to effective mediation.

- A mediator often has to be a negotiation coach, helping parties improve their relationship and communication, encouraging them to disclose interests and generate options, assisting their reality-testing by exploring alternatives and employing legitimacy information, and facilitating their making commitments to clear and feasible agreements.

- Similarly, a negotiator can benefit from thinking like a mediator, which helps enable the negotiator to see things from the other side's perspective and think about approaching the issues in terms of joint problem solving, rather than one side competing against the other.

Because of this close interrelatedness, and the opportunity to draw insights from one process that may be helpful in illuminating the other, we believe it is instructive and useful to cover both approaches together.

JAMES R. HOLBROOK
BENJAMIN J. COOK

April 2013

SUMMARY OF CONTENTS

TABLE OF CONTENTS

ADVANCED NEGOTIATION AND MEDIATION

CONCEPTS, SKILLS, AND EXERCISES

INTRODUCTION

■ ■ ■

In April 2011, Apple Inc., maker of the iPhone and iPad, filed a lawsuit against Samsung Electronics, claiming that Samsung had violated several of Apple's patents. Samsung countersued, contending that Apple had violated Samsung patents. On August 24, 2012, the jury found in favor of Apple and awarded the company damages of $1.05 billion. As is typical in litigation, the verdict was far from the end of the dispute. Samsung quickly announced its intention to appeal as far as the Supreme Court if necessary, and filed a motion to remove an injunction on one of its products. Apple filed requests for permanent injunctions on several of Samsung's smartphones. Samsung's appeal cannot occur until all of these motions are settled, after which the appeals process could take 9 to 12 months or even longer.

Prior to handing the case to the jury, the judge requested that both sides meet to talk one more time to try to settle their dispute, warning lawyers representing the two companies that there were risks for both sides. Indeed, despite Apple's winning this particular battle, the larger war continues and, as the judge warned, both companies still face significant risks. For Apple, the appeal could mean that the damages award is reduced or, more significantly, the decision is overturned. Even if the decision is affirmed, the legal costs of pursuing litigation will be substantial—some legal analysts have estimated dollar amounts in the hundreds of millions. For Samsung, there is a chance that the damages it must pay are even higher (the jury found that the patent infringement was deliberate, so Apple may be entitled to request treble damages) and, regardless, the legal costs of continuing to appeal will be significant. Further complicating matters for both sides, the two companies have lawsuits pending against each other in several other countries around the world, which increases the likelihood of inconsistent results across the various jurisdictions.

Sometimes litigation is the most appropriate means for resolving certain disputes. In this case, perhaps, pursuing the lengthy and costly process will provide Apple with an outcome with which it is highly satisfied, and Samsung may be content that at least it had its day in court. But it is worth considering, what if the two sides had been committed to resolving the dispute either through direct negotiation or through mediation? When prior settlement attempts failed, what were the barriers that prevented the parties from coming to an agreement? Were there additional negotiation tools that each side might have employed that would have helped overcome their impasse?

1

While not all disputes can be resolved through negotiation and mediation, far too many conflicts result in less-satisfactory outcomes—either because parties fail to try these forms of dispute resolution or, when attempted, they are done ineffectively. This book broadens understanding of negotiation and mediation as means for creating deals and resolving disputes, and provides tools for effective practice. A large amount of excellent writing in this field is available, and this book not only integrates some of that material into one place, but also examines negotiation and mediation through the framework of four distinct strategies—performative, transformative, integrative, and distributive—an approach that is unique and, we believe, highly useful to the study and practice of dispute resolution.

CHAPTER 1

WHAT IS CONFLICT?

■ ■ ■

Conflict is pervasive. Whether large or small, between individuals or organizations, short- or long-term, or however it is shaped and defined by a range of other characteristics, conflict presents both a challenge and opportunity:

- A challenge, because too often people lack the knowledge and skills to resolve conflict in an effective and constructive way.
- An opportunity, because when approached skillfully, the resolution of conflict can lead to positive, productive, and successful outcomes.

Because both negotiation and mediation can be effective approaches to resolving or mitigating various types of conflict, defining and having a basic understanding of conflict are important starting points.

1. DEFINITION

Basic definitions of conflict range from descriptions of physical interaction, such as "fight," "battle," and "opposing action of incompatibles," to less tangible confrontations, such as a "mental struggle resulting from . . . opposing needs, drives, [and] wishes."[1] Other definitions can be more expansive: "Conflict presupposes the existence of at least one difference and two identities, one on either side of a difference," and includes competition for scarce resources and the existence and operation of power.[2] While conflict is often considered negative—something to be resolved or avoided—the existence of conflict, especially when dealt with productively, can be a very effective agent for positive change and progress.

2. LEVELS OF CONFLICT

Conflict can occur at various levels. The following are commonly identified as four levels at which conflict takes place:[3]

1. **Intrapersonal**: conflict that occurs within an individual. Our own thoughts, ideas, emotions, etc., are in conflict with each oth-

---

[1] MERRIAM–WEBSTER'S DICTIONARY.

[2] Leonard C. Hawes, *Conflict and Identity,* Ron Jackson, ed., ENCYCLOPEDIA OF IDENTITY (Thousand Oaks, CA: Sage, 2010).

[3] *From* Roy J. Lewicki, Joseph A. Litterer, John W. Minton & David M. Saunders, NEGOTIATION (2nd ed.) at 5–6 (Boston: Irwin, 1994).

er. We'd like to leave the office early to spend time with friends, but we know that if we don't stay late to finish the report, tomorrow will be especially stressful.

2. **Interpersonal**: conflict that occurs between individuals. We have a heated argument with a friend over his consistent lack of punctuality, or a co-worker engages us in a contentious discussion over who should be responsible for a mistake on a joint project.

3. **Intragroup**: conflict that occurs within a small group, such as a family, class, team, committee, etc. Members of our family can't agree on where to spend Christmas vacation, or team members argue about when to meet for practice.

4. **Intergroup**: conflict that occurs between groups, such as countries, union and management, human rights groups and government, etc. A neighborhood organization protests against the city council's decision to sell wetlands to a private developer, or one country threatens to attack a neighboring country over a boundary dispute.

The concepts and skills covered in this book provide tools for more effectively analyzing and dealing with all four levels of conflict.

3.   SOURCES OF CONFLICT

Conflict can occur anywhere. Because conflict is so pervasive in daily life and can manifest itself in a vast array of situations, there is a wide range of sources to which we can look to explain the existence of conflict. The following list explores some (but by no means all) common underlying causes of conflict:[4]

- a failure of connection, collaboration, or community; an inability to understand our essential interconnectedness and the universal commonality of the human spirit;

- a lack of acceptance of ourselves that we have projected onto others; a way of blaming others for failures in our own lives;

- a boundary violation; a failure to value or recognize our own integrity or the personal space of others;

- a way of getting attention, acknowledgment, sympathy, or support by casting ourselves as the victim of some "wrongdoer;"

- the continued pursuit of our own false expectations; the desire to hold on to our unrealistic fantasies;

- a lack of listening; a failure to appreciate the nuances in what someone else is saying;

---

[4]   See generally Kenneth Cloke, MEDIATING DANGEROUSLY: THE FRONTIERS OF CONFLICT RESOLUTION (San Francisco: Jossey–Bass Publishers, 2001).

- a result of secrets, concealments, confusions, conflicting messages, cover-ups, and what we have failed to communicate;
- a lack of skill, effectiveness, or clarity in saying what we feel, think, or want;
- the urgent voice of a new paradigm; a demand for change in a system that has outlived its usefulness;
- the incomplete expression or misunderstanding of a paradox, enigma, duality, polarity, or contradiction;
- a threatened interpretation of difference, diversity, or opposition, which ignores the essential role of polarity in creating unity, balance, and symbiosis; or
- an inability to learn from past mistakes; a failure to recognize them as opportunities for growth, learning, and improved understanding.

Among all sources of conflict, identity plays an often implicit but pervasive role. Whether a dispute is simply over how much we're willing to pay for a souvenir, or what arrangements we're willing to agree with in a child custody battle, how we identify ourselves or what the issues in the dispute say about our identity are often at the heart of conflict. A challenge to our competence, integrity, or self-worth is extremely threatening and can create intense interpersonal conflict. If we agree to the seller's asking price and pay too much for the souvenir, does this mean we are less intelligent, too "soft," or generally lacking in business acumen? If we don't receive full custody of the children, does this mean we are a bad parent or that the children love us less?

People have many different identifications including, for example, cultural values, education, ethnic origin, gender, group affiliations, language and dialect, economic class, geographic location, hobbies, national citizenship, personal values, professions, race, religion, self-interests, sexual orientation, social status, wealth, etc. Two people who seem quite different thus may have many things in common and can relate to one another through their shared identifications. However, in situations of abuse of power, betrayal, blaming, discrimination, disrespect, hatred, humiliation, ignorance, intolerance, misallocation of resources, violation of rights, violence, etc., a person's multiple identifications can be collapsed into a single identity that is "miniaturized"[5] and stereotyped. This, in turn, can result in a range of manifestations of interpersonal or intergroup conflict.

---

[5] Amartya Sen, IDENTITY AND VIOLENCE: THE ILLUSION OF DESTINY at i (New York: W.W. Norton & Company, Inc., 2006).

4. RESOLVING CONFLICT

Methods for resolving conflict span a range of approaches. At a general level, conflict resolution methods can be divided into two categories: violent and non-violent. Within the non-violent category, methods fall along a spectrum, with direct negotiation on one end and trial in court on the other. The spectrum represents the amount of control parties have over both the process and the outcome, and includes mediation and other settlement processes on the nonbinding side, and various forms of arbitration and trial on the binding side (see Figure 1 below[6]).

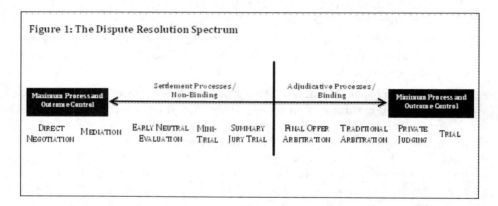

Figure 1: The Dispute Resolution Spectrum

The following are brief descriptions of the approaches along the dispute resolution spectrum in Figure 1. The list is not meant to be exhaustive—there are other forms of dispute resolution—but it does provide a representation of some of the primary approaches.

Direct negotiation: two or more parties communicate directly to resolve a dispute or create/structure a deal.

Mediation: a neutral third party intervenes to assist disputing parties in coming to an agreement by facilitating discussion and negotiation between the parties. The process is voluntary and the mediator does not have authority to impose a decision.

Early Neutral Evaluation: parties select a neutral to evaluate the strengths and weaknesses of their case and sometimes assist them in coming to an agreement by making non-binding recommendations.

Mini–Trial: parties present limited versions of their cases to an independent neutral in the presence of representatives from each side who have authority to settle. The neutral then works with both sides to facilitate an agreement.

---

[6] See generally Jay Folberg & Dwight Golann, LAWYER NEGOTIATION: THEORY, PRACTICE AND LAW (2nd ed.) (New York: Aspen Casebooks, 2010).

Summary Jury Trial: a jury is selected and a mock trial is conducted in which both parties present evidence in a summary manner. After the jury renders a verdict, the parties meet again to attempt to come to an agreement before proceeding to a court trial.

Final-Offer Arbitration: parties submit proposed final offers to an arbitrator who then chooses the offer that is closest to her evaluation of a fair outcome. The selected offer is binding.

Traditional Arbitration: parties present evidence to an arbitrator who then issues a binding decision. The process may include submission of briefs and exhibits, examination of witnesses, etc., but is less formal and more flexible than a court trial.

Private Judging: similar to a bench trial in court, in which the parties agree on an individual (often a retired judge) who hears the matter in private and renders a binding decision.

Trial: parties publicly appear before a judge and jury in court and are bound by rules of evidence and procedure; the jury hears evidence from both sides and renders a verdict, which becomes a binding judgment.

No single approach on the dispute resolution spectrum is appropriate for resolving all conflicts. (See the table below called "Evaluating ADR Processes," for an illustration of how the range of processes meets various client needs.) The nature of the conflict and a host of other factors can affect which approach is best suited for a specific dispute. However, far too many disputes follow the adjudicative path, which too often involves lengthy and costly discovery, motion practice, and trial with minimal control of process and outcome, when a more appropriate approach on the other end of the spectrum may have led to much more satisfactory results.

This book focuses on negotiation and mediation as especially effective approaches to resolving conflict. While negotiation and mediation are not always the most appropriate methods of resolving a specific conflict, they are still underutilized (or mis-utilized) approaches that, when done effectively, can lead to settlements, agreements, deals, and resolutions that are highly satisfying and successful for both parties. The theories, strategies, and tools discussed in this book are intended to enhance understanding, facilitate skills-building, and promote the effective use of negotiation and mediation.

EVALUATING ADR PROCESSES[7]

Client Objectives	Processes				
	Negotiation	Mediation	Early Neutral Evaluation	Binding Arbitration	Litigation
Minimize Cost	3	2	2	1	0
Provide Speedy Process	3	2	2	1	0
Maintain Privacy	3	3	3	3	0
Maintain/ Improve Relation- ship	3	3	1	1	0
Accomplish Mutual Needs Fulfillment	3	3	1-3	0	0
Obtain Expert Opinion	0	0-3	3	1	0-1
Obtain Enforceable Binding Decision	0	0	0	3	3
Obtain Public Precedent	0	0	0	0	3
				0 = Poor 2 = Good 1 = Fair 3 = Excellent	

---

[7]   See generally Frank E.A. Sander & Stephen B. Goldberg, *Fitting the Forum to the Fuss: A User Friendly Guide to Selecting an ADR Procedure*, 10 NEG. J. 49 (1994).

5. NAMING, BLAMING, CLAIMING, AND SO ON: A SYSTEM OF CONFLICT ESCALATION AND RESOLUTION

The authors of "The Emergence and Transformation of Disputes: Naming, Blaming, Claiming" describe a system of conflict escalation and resolution that explains the evolution of a litigated dispute from the time it is perceived by a party as significant until it is filed in court to be decided by adjudication.[8] Along this timeline of conflict escalation, parties can resolve their disputes themselves by negotiation, or they can submit their disputes to private mediation before the disputes become cases filed in court. Once disputes are filed in court, cases can be resolved by negotiation or mediation. If a court case is not settled, it will be adjudicated and decided by a jury and judge. Cases that are lost in court can be appealed.

At every point along this timeline of conflict escalation, parties are motivated by the forces of personal preferences and experience, relationships, psychology, family and social upbringing, cultural norms and values, and avoidable risks and transaction costs to resolve their conflicts and get on with their lives.

The authors contend that disputes are social constructs that evolve through specific predictable stages:

- We ignore and therefore tolerate most injurious experiences that we encounter in our lives in traffic, at work, in commercial transactions, and at home. These injurious experiences never rise to the level of becoming "conflicts."
- Injurious experiences become "conflicts" when they become significant enough for us to perceive them as unwanted and disvalued. At this point we "name" them as conflicts and they become part of our self-conscious lives (e.g., "I don't like my job").
- Conflicts escalate to become "grievances" when we "blame" a specific person for causing us a perceived injury, harm, or injustice (e.g., "I don't like my job because my boss is too demanding and doesn't pay me enough money").
- Grievances escalate to become "claims" when we demand that the person whom we perceived to have wronged us is responsible for remedying the harm (e.g., I tell my boss, "You need to assign me less work and pay me more money").
- Claims escalate to become "disputes" when our demands for a remedy are rejected in whole or in part by the person we deem to be responsible for the harm (e.g., my boss tells me, "If you don't

---

[8] See generally William L.F. Felstiner, Richard L. Abel, & Austin Sarat, "The Emergence and Transformation of Disputes: Naming, Blaming, Claiming. . .," 15 LAW & SOCIETY REV. 631–54 (1980–81).

like working here for what I pay you, you can quit and I'll hire someone else").

- Disputes escalate to become "lawsuits" when we engage lawyers to reframe these rejected claims into legally cognizable causes of action and file them as cases to be decided in court (e.g., my lawyer states in a complaint in court that my boss pays me less than his young American Caucasian Christian male employees because I am an older African Muslim woman from Mali, and my boss is engaging in unlawful age, racial, religious, gender, and ethnic discrimination).

So, on the timeline of conflict escalation, unperceived injurious experiences become conflicts when we give them names; conflicts become grievances when we blame a specific person for injuring us; grievances become claims when we demand that the person remedy the harm; claims become disputes when the person refuses to remedy the harm; and disputes become lawsuits when lawyers reframe disputes as legally cognizable causes of action filed in court.

We also can imagine the timeline of conflict escalation as having the shape of a pyramid. At the bottom of the pyramid are the many troubles, problems, and personal and social upsets which are everyday occurrences that we ignore and tolerate as unperceived injurious experiences. These injurious experiences go unnamed and therefore do not ripen into conflicts.

At the next level up the pyramid, injurious experiences ripen into conflicts when we name them as unwanted.

At the next level up the pyramid, conflicts become grievances when we blame a specific person for harming us.

At the next level up the pyramid, grievances become claims when we demand that the person remedy our injury. Because often we express our grievances only to intimates, and not to the person whom we blame, most grievances do not ripen into claims.

At the next level up the pyramid, claims become disputes when the person who harmed us rejects our demands for a remedy. Because some claims are accepted and remedied by the wrongdoer, or because we decide not to pursue a claim any further, only a small fraction of injurious experiences ever mature from rejected claims into disputes.

At the next level up the pyramid, some disputes become lawsuits because they are significant enough that we engage lawyers to file our disputes in court. Because the transactional costs of litigation (including time, money, hassle, and uncertainty) are substantial, the vast majority of cases (e.g., about 98% of civil cases) filed in court never go to trial.

At the top of the pyramid are the lawsuits, which are lost in court which are appealed. Because the transactional costs of an appeal are substantial, most cases lost in court are never appealed.

There are numerous important lessons to be learned from this conflict escalation and resolution theory:

1.　Most injurious experiences never mature into conflicts; most conflicts never mature into grievances; most grievances never mature into claims; most claims never mature into disputes; most disputes never mature into lawsuits; and most unsuccessful lawsuits never mature into appeals.

2.　Parties are psychologically and socially incentivized to tolerate conflicts.

3.　Parties are economically incentivized not to escalate grievances into claims.

4.　Parties are economically incentivized to avoid asserting frivolous claims, which are highly likely to be rejected.

5.　Parties are economically incentivized to resolve meritorious claims by pre-litigation negotiation or mediation and thereby avoid the transactional costs of disputes maturing into lawsuits.

6.　Courts are incentivized by docket management concerns to order parties to submit appropriate cases to mediation.

7.　Parties are economically incentivized to participate in good faith in court-annexed mediation to settle their lawsuits and thereby minimize the transactional costs of litigation.

This conflict escalation and resolution system is affected at every point by personal preferences and experience, relationships, psychology, family and social upbringing, cultural norms and values, and an unavoidable economic cost/benefit/risk/reward calculus. These forces either cause us to stop where we are on the conflict escalation timeline and enable us to choose to accept, resolve, and tolerate the level of conflict we experience, or the forces drive us farther along the conflict escalation timeline from conflicts, to grievances, to claims, to disputes, to lawsuits, and ultimately to appeals.

One intuitive argument that can be made about such a conflict escalation and resolution system is: the more inefficient the conflict resolution system is (i.e., the fewer disputes the system resolves), the fewer perceived injurious experiences will be filed as lawsuits in court. This is the argument sometimes heard in countries where the huge backlog of cases in courts discourages disputes from being filed as lawsuits (e.g., India, numerous African and South American countries, etc.).

A second but counter-intuitive argument that can be made about such a conflict escalation and resolution system is: the more efficient the conflict resolution system is (i.e., the more disputes the system resolves), the more perceived injurious experiences will be filed as lawsuits in court. This is the argument sometimes heard in India—that the success of court-annexed mediation there will be socially perceived as reducing the backlog of cases in Indian courts, thereby encouraging more disputes to be filed as lawsuits.

Mediators can intervene in this system of conflict escalation and resolution to encourage and empower parties to consider personal preferences and experience, relationships, psychology, family and social upbringing, cultural norms and values, and avoidable risks and transaction costs. These forces can motivate disputants to choose to accept, resolve, and tolerate the level of conflict they experience and thereby enable them to get on with their lives.

A. AN INTRODUCTION TO FOUR KINDS OF NEGOTIATION

Most negotiation courses teach two negotiation strategies: distributive and integrative. In addition to these two kinds of negotiation, we cover two more negotiation strategies: performative and transformative. We also treat common positional bargaining behaviors as a subset of performative negotiation, rather than as a form of distributive negotiation, which has an integral, economics-driven theory and unique related concepts and skills. We believe negotiators need to use all the effective techniques at their disposal and flexibly employ appropriate negotiation principles as needed to achieve the outcomes they desire. As negotiators understand when and how to use these four different sets of negotiation principles systematically, they wield more powerful tools to close deals and settle disputes effectively.

The next section introduces and briefly describes the four kinds of negotiation.

A Day in the Negotiation Life of Joe Carter

In the opening pages of their book, NEGOTIATION,[9] the authors Lewicki, Litterer, Minton, and Saunders describe a day in the negotiation life of Joe Carter. During the course of one day, Carter encounters four different negotiation situations,[10] which together involve all four negotiation strategies covered in this book.

1. TRANSFORMATIVE NEGOTIATION

The first situation involves negotiation of a strong difference of opinion between Carter and his wife about where they want to go for vacation.

---

[9]   Lewicki, Litterer, Minton & Saunders, NEGOTIATION (2nd ed.) at 2–3.

[10]   They also identify a fifth, multi-party, public-conflict dispute resolution context, which is not the subject of our book.

Joe wants them to charter a sailboat and cruise New England coastal waters. Sue wants them to go on her college's alumni-sponsored tour of the Far East. They don't want to take separate vacations, but neither wants to concede to the other's preference. To choose either the sailing vacation or the touring vacation will leave one spouse unhappy. They don't have the time, money, or shared interests to both sail the New England coast and tour the Far East together, which also is a compromise that would satisfy neither spouse. This vacation-planning conflict therefore has become a conflict that is adversely affecting their relationship.

The central issue in a transformative negotiation context involves the parties' relationship (e.g., whether and how to create a relationship, maintain it, change it, end it, or replace it with a new and different kind of relationship). The authors Bush and Folger[11] contend that this kind of negotiation presents opportunities for both "empowerment" and "recognition." The parties can help one another clarify goals, options, and resources, and then they can make informed, deliberate, and free choices regarding how to proceed. Bush and Folger believe that a successful transformative approach also "will bring out the intrinsic strength and goodness that lie within the parties as human beings"[12]

2.   INTEGRATIVE NEGOTIATION

The second negotiation situation from the Joe Carter scenario involves a dispute between two departments at work. Carter is the head of his company's engineering design group. In the company parking lot that morning, Carter encounters the head of the purchasing department. They need to talk about a problem dealing with company vendors. The purchasing department wants all contacts with vendors to go through them. The engineers need technical information from vendors, but they can't readily get this information when going through the purchasing department. The company's senior management expects the two department managers to solve this problem, and Carter believes he and the head of the purchasing department can sit down together, talk this through, and work out a mutually acceptable solution.

The central issue in an integrative negotiation context involves creative problem-solving that achieves a mutually acceptable joint solution. An integrative approach, according to Bush and Folger, enables parties to seek comprehensive solutions to mutually defined problems. By using openness, collaboration, and creativity, parties can work together to ex-

---

[11]   Robert A. Baruch Bush & Joseph P. Folger, THE PROMISE OF MEDIATION: RESPONDING TO CONFLICT THROUGH EMPOWERMENT AND RECOGNITION (San Francisco: Jossey–Bass Publishers, 1994).

[12]   *Id.* at 95.

pand resources, create rather than claim value, and address each others' needs as the best way to address one's own needs.[13]

3. DISTRIBUTIVE NEGOTIATION

The third negotiation situation in Carter's day involves a telephone call about an ongoing conversation that Carter is having with a salesman at an automobile dealership about the price of a luxury car that Carter is interested in buying. Carter is pleased with the salesman's last offer, but Sue thinks the car is too expensive. Carter tells the salesman about Sue's concern to try to influence the salesman to make an even lower offer, one that may be acceptable to Sue as a related third-party decisionmaker in this negotiation.

The central issue in a distributive negotiation context is the acceptable exchange of value (e.g., here, the exchange of money for a car). Bush and Folger describe this as the zero-sum sorting-out of competing claims for value, according to principles of power, rights, or fairness. This kind of negotiation underlies many market-based transactions and much of formal legal dispute resolution.[14]

4. PERFORMATIVE NEGOTIATION

The fourth negotiation situation that Carter encounters involves another dispute inside the company, this time with the finance department about the annual budget process, which has caused a huge unresolved argument. The finance department has reduced Carter's engineering design group's proposed budget by 30 percent, which cuts out funds for development of new projects for the coming year. Carter regards the company's finance people as arrogant and arbitrary, and he is prepared to draw the line and continue fighting with them about the budget cuts.

The central issue in a performative negotiation context is improving the parties' communication, which is often polarized, adversarial, and positional. According to Bush and Folger, these kinds of conflicts tend to make parties feel threatened, victimized, vulnerable, out of control, fearful, confused, and unsure of what to do. This makes a party defensive, suspicious, and hostile to the other party, which makes it difficult for the parties to look beyond their own individual interests.[15]

Using All Four Kinds of Negotiation Principles in One Negotiation

While the Joe Carter example illustrates four different negotiation scenarios, often two or more of the four negotiation strategies are at play in a

---

[13] *Id.* at 57–58.

[14] *Id.* at 57.

[15] *Id.* at 191.

single negotiation setting. For example, a negotiation between divorcing parents who want to be effective co-parents probably will require use of all four kinds of negotiation:

- To get beyond blaming and victimization to communicate more effectively, they will need to use performative negotiation principles.

- To move beyond the bitter feelings of divorce and create a new, mutually supportive co-parenting relationship, they will need to use transformative negotiation principles.

- To cooperatively and creatively address custody, visitation, and a host of other mutual-problem issues, they will need to use integrative negotiation principles.

- To fairly resolve disputes about alimony or child support, they will need to use distributive negotiation principles.

5.   THE FOUR STRATEGIES APPLIED: NEGOTIATING AND MEDIATING A PHYSICIAN–PATIENT CONFLICT[16]

The following account describes a conflict between a physician and patient, followed by an analysis of the dispute using the four strategies in both negotiation and mediation.

The Patient's Story:

> *I was around six to ten weeks pregnant when I had my first visit with Dr. Obg who had been my gynecologist for years. On the Thursday morning of my appointment, I started experiencing abdominal pain. Dr. Obg told me she thought I was undergoing a miscarriage, and I was given a shot of methotrexate. I was told there would be pain; I was told that I would be uncomfortable, but it would make the pregnancy terminate; and I was told I didn't need to worry about anything else. I was given a prescription for pain killers in case the pain got really bad.*

> *On Saturday evening at home, I had sudden shooting pains in my lower abdomen. The pain was so bad, it dropped me to my knees, and I started to throw up and shake. I thought that this was a side effect of the methotrexate, so I took a pain pill and, when the pain subsided, I fell asleep. On Sunday I was still uncomfortable. Again, I took another pain killer so I could relax. On Monday, I saw Dr. Obg who said the pain was from the methotrexate, the pain was normal, and it would be controlled by the pain pills. On Tuesday, when I again felt pain, I called her and she said the same thing.*

> *On Wednesday I called Dr. Obg's nurse and told her I was going to the ER at the hospital because I couldn't stand the pain. The ER doc-*

---

[16] See generally James R. Holbrook, *Negotiating, Mediating, and Arbitrating Physician–Patient Conflicts,* CLINICAL OBSTETRICS AND GYNECOLOGY 719–30 (December 2008).

tor called Dr. Obg and told her I was there. Dr.Obg told him to send me home with additional pain killers and that I would be fine.

On Thursday I went to see Dr. Obg. She sat across the room from me with my patient folder in her lap. She looked at me like I was crying wolf. She explained to me that "everyone has different pain tolerances" and maybe mine was low. I told her my pain tolerance is high, and what was happening to me now wasn't normal. She told me that she would examine me again if I wanted her to, but that nothing would be different. I sat there and cried; she dismissed me and I went home.

On Friday evening I went to the ER again and was given an ultra-sound. Within minutes I was told I was bleeding internally and that I needed immediate surgery. I was diagnosed with a ruptured ectopic pregnancy. The corrective surgery didn't take long and I was out of the hospital within 24 hours. My right fallopian tube was removed. My physical condition was terrible, but my emotional condition was much worse. Apparently I have endometriosis that was never diagnosed by Dr. Obg after years of going to see her. I really want her to apologize, because this shouldn't have happened to me. I believed in her and she let me down. If she had been supportive and kind, then maybe the entire experience would have been different.

The patient's story reveals anger, blame, confusion, fear, frustration, and a profound sense of abandonment, betrayal, and victimization, plus a somewhat-muted desire for revenge. These characteristics are quite common when a person is in the midst of unresolved conflict:

> Involvement in conflict affects all parties in similar ways. No matter what the context, disputes make parties feel fearful, confused, and unsure of what to do. As a result, they feel vulnerable and out of control. Moreover, in the heat of conflict, disputing parties typically feel threatened or victimized by the conduct and claims of the other party. As a result, they are defensive, suspicious, and hostile to the other party, and almost incapable of looking beyond their own needs. Thus, across all contexts, conflicts engender in people the experience of relative weakness and relative self-absorption.[17]

The possibility that a physician may have committed an error, especially when confronted with the patient's accusation that the physician is indifferent and uncaring, challenges the physician's identity for competence, integrity, and self-worth.[18] This challenge to the physician's professional identity is extremely threatening. The perception of this threat can provoke the physician to become defensive and self-protective,

---

[17]   Robert A. Baruch Bush & Joseph P. Folger, THE PROMISE OF MEDIATION: RESPONDING TO CONFLICT THROUGH EMPOWERMENT AND RECOGNITION 191 (San Francisco: Jossey–Bass Publishers, 1994).

[18]   *See* Douglas Stone, Bruce Patton & Sheila Heen, DIFFICULT CONVERSATIONS: HOW TO DISCUSS WHAT MATTERS MOST 109–117 (New York: Penguin Books, 2000).

withdraw, rationalize her withdrawal, and even blame the patient, e.g., for being difficult.[19]

6. NEGOTIATING THE PHYSICIAN–PATIENT CONFLICT

What makes negotiation so difficult to use for resolving this physician-patient conflict are the heightened emotions of both participants and their understandable desire to avoid a painful conversation about what happened and who is to blame. Therefore, the first (and most difficult) step is for Dr. Obg and her patient to agree to meet and listen to what each party has to say. This is easier said than done.

People in high-conflict situations typically create and tell stories which present each speaker's one-sided perspective of what is "true."[20] Because these stories are not intended to be fair, complete, or accurate descriptions of both sides of the conflict, conflict stories often conceal face-threatening facts, feelings, and identity issues affecting the speaker. Conflict stories cast the speaker as victim (or hero) and cast all the blame on the other party as the wrongdoer. Conflict stories focus on the past (blaming), and not on the present (problem-solving). Although the speaker may want to tell her story to the other person, she does not want to listen to, acknowledge, or be persuaded by what the other person has to say.

This means that, if Dr. Obg and her patient somehow became willing to sit together and talk about what happened, the nature of and their responses to their respective conflict stories would make negotiating a mutually acceptable resolution of their conflict very difficult. As each party told her story, the other likely would become more threatened, more defensive, and more self-protective. This negatively reactive cycle typically leads to a so-called "death spiral" of arguing, name-calling, shouting or sulking, and finally walking out in a huff. It is important to note, however, that this kind of verbal fighting, exchanging angry words, blaming one another, defending oneself, etc., is a form of negotiation which we call performative negotiation.

Performative negotiation often involves simultaneous speeches (talking over each other) or overlapping speeches (interrupting each other), but seldom involves sequenced speeches (taking turns talking and listening). The parties in such a high-conflict negotiation often do not understand that they are arguing, not about the same reality, but rather about their differing perceptions of what is real, which also is colored by their anger

---

[19] *See* Jerome Groopman, M.D., HOW DOCTORS THINK 264–65 (New York: Houghton Mifflin Company, 2007).

[20] *See generally* Kenneth Cloke & Joan Goldsmith, RESOLVING PERSONAL AND ORGANIZATIONAL CONFLICT: STORIES OF TRANSFORMATION AND FORGIVENESS (San Francisco: Jossey–Bass Publishers, 2000).

and other negative emotions. Their views of each other frequently are based on conclusions or assumptions (often unstated or maybe even unrecognized) rather than on accurate observations which they share in common. Trying to determine the "truth" about what happened, or "who started it" or "where or when it all began" or who is "right" and who is "to blame" often has little or no practical value in resolving the conflict. Questions about these things often protract the conflict and provoke even more defensiveness.

Performative negotiation is helpful by creating face time in which the parties can tell their conflict stories to one another. This is best done when the parties can avoid threatening each other's identity, control the expression of their own negative emotions, and agree to take turns talking and listening. It also may include the parties asking and answering questions of one another, disclosing additional information, or obtaining needed information.

After expressing and listening to each other's conflict stories, Dr. Obg and her patient may be willing to engage in transformative negotiation to empathetically end or repair their damaged relationship; or they could use integrative negotiation to work together to agree about what they want to do together now; or they could use distributive negotiation to prudently terminate their relationship and move on with their lives separately.

By using transformative negotiation, Dr. Obg may feel more empathy for her patient and recognize that she contributed to the problem by the ways in which she misdiagnosed the patient's condition and ignored or dismissed the patient's concerns. Her patient can be empowered to no longer feel like a victim and thus feel she can make appropriate choices about how to move on with her life and make future healthcare decisions. Whether Dr. Obg and the patient decide to continue or terminate their relationship, they may do so with better feelings on both sides.

By using integrative negotiation, Dr. Obg and her patient could focus on their self-interests and possible ways in which they might work together cooperatively to maximize their respective interests. Dr. Obg does not want to be accused of committing malpractice and she does not want her patient to impugn her reputation in the community. The patient does not want to feel abandoned or disrespected by Dr. Obg. They could agree (perhaps somewhat warily) to continue their relationship upon their mutual commitment that they will immediately discuss with one another any future concerns or disagreements about the patient's condition or care.

By using distributive negotiation, Dr. Obg could offer her patient an apology or agree to refund insurance co-payments in exchange for a formal written release from the patient of all claims of malpractice. This probably would result in a permanent termination of the physician-patient relationship, with unresolved bad feelings continuing on both sides.

7.   MEDIATING THE PHYSICIAN–PATIENT CONFLICT

For the reasons discussed above, it is understandable that Dr. Obg and her patient are unlikely to agree to confront one another face to face and attempt to negotiate a resolution of their conflict. Something more is needed to help both parties feel safe enough to meet and talk about what happened. Mediation can be both a safe container for such a meeting and a helpful catalyst for resolution. An impartial third-party mediator can host a respectful problem-solving process. An experienced mediator often has expertise in the subject matter of the dispute. (Here, the dispute involves the breakdown of communication between a physician and her patient that results in the patient's perception that she was harmed by her doctor whom she trusted for many years.) The mediator can structure the way the parties tell their conflict stories so as to productively manage the parties' expression of strong negative emotions. The mediator can help the parties take turns talking and listening, asking and answering questions of one another, disclosing additional information, or obtaining needed information. The mediator can help the parties focus on their self-interests and possible ways in which the parties might work together cooperatively to maximize their respective interests. The mediator can help the parties seek opportunities for empowerment and recognition. If appropriate, the mediator can help the parties either repair or end their relationship in a mutually respectful manner. In this regard, the mediator can help the parties find, agree on, and use objective standards of fairness to reach closure and move on with their lives.

Overarching everything else, the mediator is committed and required to keep everything about the mediation confidential from outside parties, and to protect the confidential nature of information which one party shares with the mediator (usually in a private caucus) that she does not want disclosed to the other party.

The parties here have several practical considerations about which they must agree, including: who is going to be the mediator; what specific roles is the mediator authorized to play; and who is going to pay for the mediator's fees and expenses? The mediator could be an employee of Dr. Obg's medical group or an ombudsperson at the hospital. However, the patient is not likely to feel that such a mediator can be impartial. The mediator could be someone who has served as the mediator in other conflicts involving Dr. Obg with other patients, but the patient here may feel that such a "repeat player" could be biased in favor of Dr. Obg.

Assuming that Dr. Obg and her patient agree on who will serve as their mediator, there are various roles that the mediator can play in the mediation. First, the mediator can be "facilitative" and help the parties improve the quality and quantity of their communication and their negotiation. Second, the mediator can be "analytical" and ask both parties questions (usually in private caucuses) that require them to focus on the benefits of reaching resolution as well as the risks of failing to reach agreement. Third, the parties may want the mediator (later in the mediation and only to help break an impasse) to be "evaluative" and share information or express opinions about the merits of the conflict and what might happen to the parties if they fail to reach agreement. Fourth, the parties also may want the mediator (only late in the mediation and only to help break an impasse) to be "directive" and tell the parties what they should do to resolve their conflict (see Chapter 2 for more discussion of the four mediation styles).

The mediation literature regards a mediator's "facilitative" and "analytical" roles as part of mainstream mediation. However, there is a dispute about whether mediators also should be "evaluative" or "directive." Some commentators believe that an "evaluative" role is not part of mediation, but rather is more akin to an ADR process called "early neutral evaluation" where an expert is hired by parties in conflict for the purpose of expressing the expert's opinions about the merits of the conflict and what is likely to happen to the parties if they fail to reach agreement. Similarly, these same commentators believe that a "directive" role is not part of mediation, but rather is more akin to an ADR process called "non-binding arbitration" in which the parties hire an expert to hear evidence about their dispute, decide who is the winner, and also decide what the loser is supposed to do. The parties are free either to accept the non-binding "award" or ignore it.

Despite disagreements about what roles a mediator should play, mediators in the marketplace of mediation often are hired because they are willing and are regarded by the parties as competent to be evaluative and directive, if necessary, to help the parties overcome an impasse late in the mediation process. Because the conflict between Dr. Obg and her patient involves allegations of medical malpractice, Dr. Obg probably would be represented by counsel during the mediation. If so, her lawyer may want the mediator to be experienced in mediating medical malpractice disputes. Dr. Obg's lawyer also may want the mediator to be competent and willing to be evaluative and even directive, in the event the parties reach an impasse late in the mediation.

EXERCISE

Analyze an important negotiation in which you participated and identify what negotiation strategies were used by the parties. How did these strategies affect the parties' communication and the outcome of the negotiation?

B. INTRODUCTION TO THE HARVARD NEGOTIATION PROJECT'S SEVEN ELEMENTS OF NEGOTIATION

Members of the Harvard Negotiation Project have observed that every negotiation, regardless of subject matter or strategy, has seven structural elements ("the Seven Elements"):[21]

RELATIONSHIP: Two (or more) negotiators must deal with one another while negotiating, even if this is a one-time transaction and they have no past or ongoing interaction. Relationship issues in negotiation include:

- How can the negotiators create an effective working relationship?

- How can the negotiators deal with their differences productively?

- How can the negotiators separate their egos from the issues in dispute?

COMMUNICATION: The negotiators must talk to each other while negotiating. Communication issues in negotiation include:

- How can the negotiators talk with each other more effectively and productively?

- How can each negotiator be a better listener?

- What information do the negotiators need to learn from each another?

INTERESTS: The negotiators are negotiating because each has concerns, objectives, needs, desires, or fears they want to have satisfied in some way, whether or not they disclose their interests directly to one another during the negotiation. Interest issues in negotiation include:

- What are the negotiators' important needs and concerns?

- Should the negotiators disclose their interests to one other?

---

[21] *See, e.g.*, Roger Fisher & Daniel Shapiro, BEYOND REASON: USING EMOTIONS AS YOU NEGOTIATE at 9 (New York: Viking, 2005); Bruce Patton, *Negotiation*, THE HANDBOOK OF DISPUTE RESOLUTION AT 279–85 (SAN FRANCISCO: JOSSEY–BASS PUBLISHERS, 2005); AND ROGER FISHER & DANNY ERTEL, Getting Ready to Negotiate (NEW YORK: PENGUIN BOOKS, 1995).

- How do the negotiators deal with incompatible interests?

OPTIONS: There are various possible ways negotiators might work together so their interests can be more-or-less satisfied in a negotiated agreement. Option issues in negotiation include:

- How can negotiators work effectively together to identify and create multiple options?

- How do negotiators use their respective important interests to invent options that might be mutually acceptable?

- How can negotiators improve an acceptable option?

LEGITIMACY: There are objective standards (e.g., market value, precedents, industry practices) and fair procedures (e.g., appraisals, bidding, split-the-difference) that negotiators can use to evaluate and select options. Legitimacy issues in negotiation include:

- Can each negotiator identify an applicable precedent, appraisal, industry standard, etc., to use to evaluate options during the negotiation?

- Should (and can) the negotiators agree on one legitimacy principle they both will use to evaluate options?

- If there is an impasse, can the negotiators agree on how they will obtain a legitimacy principle they both will use to try to overcome the impasse?

ALTERNATIVES: If no agreement is reached in negotiation, there are possible things a negotiator can do away from the table without the other negotiator's agreement. Of these various alternatives, one is called the Best Alternative to a Negotiated Agreement (BATNA) which can be attractive (a strong BATNA) or unattractive (a weak BATNA) to pursue. Issues involving alternatives in negotiation include:

- What is each negotiator's realistic BATNA?

- How strong or weak is each negotiator's BATNA?

> - Should a negotiator disclose her BATNA during the negotiation? If so, how and when?

COMMITMENT: This includes any pre-conditions of the negotiators that must be met to negotiate, plus the negotiators' ability and willingness to assent to and comply with their negotiated agreement. Commitment issues in negotiation include:

> - Who are the necessary parties that must be involved in the negotiation?
>
> - Does each negotiator have authority to enter into a final, binding agreement?
>
> - Will the parties comply with the terms of the final agreement?

The Seven Elements are especially useful in preparing for negotiation.[22] Negotiators are more likely to be effective when they consider each element, contemplate how each relates to their particular situation, and thoroughly plan how to account for or integrate the elements into their negotiation. The Seven Elements also are useful in analyzing an ineffective negotiation and diagnosing the problems that are occurring which might be fixed.

The following is a brief look at how each element relates to and affects a negotiation.

1. ENHANCING RELATIONSHIPS IN NEGOTIATION

Knowing the other negotiator personally, or at least by reputation, is helpful. You know whether and how much you can trust the other person. You have a better sense of how she sees the world, how she prefers to be treated, and what might influence her. It also is easier to communicate with someone you know. It is easier to talk about and move beyond personal or substantive difficulties in the negotiation when you know the other negotiator.

When negotiating with a stranger, it can be useful to look for common experiences, similar hobbies or personal interests, and shared opinions. These commonalities tend to help the negotiators feel better about one another and make them more willing to listen to each other.

The relationship between negotiators can be enhanced by consistently showing courtesy and respect, doing a favor, immediately returning a favor, making a concession, disclosing some relevant information, allowing

---

[22] *See, e.g.*, Roger Fisher & Danny Ertel, GETTING READY TO NEGOTIATE (New York: Penguin Books, 1995).

the other negotiator to "save face" especially in front of her client, helping her avoid being caught by surprise, etc.

The seating arrangement in a negotiation also can help enhance a negotiating relationship, e.g., by sitting side-by-side or facing a whiteboard or flipchart that outlines the agenda of issues to be negotiated. This helps make it clear that the dispute or transaction being negotiated is a mutual problem to be mutually resolved, rather than an interpersonal conflict about which the negotiators must contend. This also makes it clear that the other negotiator is not the problem, but actually is an essential part of the negotiating relationship needed to solve the problem.

"Trust" in a negotiation is a function of the quality of the negotiators' communication and relationship. Trust refers to one negotiator's expectation that the other negotiator will (1) disclose necessary, accurate, relevant information and (2) consistently work to maintain and enhance the negotiators' relationship. An increased level of trust in the negotiators' relationship increases the likelihood they can successfully utilize an integrative negotiation strategy, whereas a decreased level of trust decreases the likelihood they can successfully engage in integrative negotiation. If there is no trust between the negotiators, they likely will use distributive negotiation or even default into performative negotiation. Similarly, if the negotiators must deal with each other in future negotiations, they are more likely to treat each other in a trustworthy manner, whereas if they need never deal with each other again, there is less relationship-related incentive to be trustworthy.

2.   IMPROVING COMMUNICATION IN NEGOTIATION

Experience tells us that, to be better communicators, we must be better listeners. Listening enables us to understand the other negotiator's perceptions, emotions, word choices, needs, and constraints. By demonstrating that you understand the other negotiator and acknowledge what she is saying, both factually and emotionally, you increase her willingness to listen to you, to be less defensive, and even to be more reasonable, at least on some issues.

Listening effectively involves using four kinds of communicative behaviors:

1.   Attending Behaviors:
     * Maintain appropriate posture and proximity to the other person.
     * Make empathic eye contact and empathic facial expressions.
     * Use encouraging non-verbal expressions (e.g., head nodding).

2.   Inviting Behaviors:
     * Listen without interrupting, judging, or preparing to talk.

- Use encouraging verbal expressions (e.g., "uh-huh," "okay," "I see").
- Encourage the other person to continue talking (e.g., "tell me more about . . .").

3. Confirming Behaviors:
   - Ask follow-up questions with sincere curiosity to get additional information.
   - Show that you understand the other person's feelings (i.e., her emotional affect).
   - Acknowledge that you find something of merit in what you have heard.

4. Summarizing Behaviors:
   - Briefly summarize what you have heard, using the other negotiator's key words and feelings.
   - Ask whether your summary is correct and complete.
   - Revise your summary, if necessary, and demonstrate that your understanding is now correct and complete.

Acknowledging that you understand the other negotiator can be challenging because of your fear the other negotiator will misinterpret your understanding as your substantive agreement with her. Therefore, we must be clear that understanding and agreement are two very different things, i.e., understanding does not equal agreement.

Although the need to be a good listener in negotiation is essential, it is difficult to listen effectively, especially in the middle of a stressful or adversarial negotiation. Particularly then, we must remind ourselves to pay close attention to the other negotiator's opinions and point of view. It is to our advantage to understand what the other negotiator really wants, which may be masked by her statement of her position.

Negotiators often respond to what they dislike in the other negotiator's position or proposal and ignore things they like. This provokes negative emotions and substantive opposition. It is more useful to identify areas of agreement, areas of disagreement, and areas of irrelevance that can be ignored. Negotiators also may disagree about differing conclusions or assumptions, whereas they may agree about the facts underlying their conclusions or assumptions. Similarly, it is more useful to talk about interests and reasoning than to argue about disputed facts. Because negotiators often disagree about what happened in the past (especially about who is to blame), it is useful to shift the time frame of the negotiation from past to present and talk about what they want to do about the problem and what they are willing to do now. Often, it is not necessary to insist on reaching complete agreement about what happened in the past to begin problem solving in the present.

3.   IDENTIFYING INTERESTS IN NEGOTIATION

Interests include positive and negative objectives, needs, desires, concerns, fears, aversions, and the like. They may be substantive or procedural in nature. Substantive interests include objective interests which are tangible, quantitative, and rational (e.g., a party's desire to get a sum of money), and subjective interests which are intangible, qualitative, and emotional (e.g., a party's desire to get an apology). Procedural interests are those related to being treated with courtesy and respect, disclosing and obtaining relevant information, using performative, transformative, integrative, or distributive principles to achieve an acceptable outcome, or employing objective standards of legitimacy and fairness. Interests may also relate to third parties (e.g., family members, friends, or co-workers) who are affected by, but are not directly involved in, a transaction or dispute.

The negotiators' underlying interests frequently are embedded in or obscured by the positions they assert early in a negotiation which, therefore, must be uncovered during the negotiation. The authors Fisher, Ury, and Patton emphasize that, "In searching for the basic interests behind a declared position, look particularly for those bedrock concerns which motivate all people. If you can take care of such basic needs, you increase the chance both of reaching agreement and, if an agreement is reached, of the other side's keeping to it."[23] They identify these basic human needs as security, economic well-being, a sense of belonging, the desire for recognition, and having control over one's life.

In discussing interests concealed by positions, Fisher and Ertel give the example of a seller's demand that he must be paid in cash.[24] This demand is a negotiating position, not an interest. To identify the interest underlying the position, the buyer can ask the seller a direct question such as, "For what purpose do you need to be paid in cash?" or the buyer can ask an indirect question such as, "Help me understand why you need to be paid in cash." The seller's answers to the buyer's interest-identification questions may reveal that the seller's underlying interest is that she wants certainty and that she will be fully paid, and incur no risk of non-payment and have no potential for economic loss.

Similarly, in a construction contract negotiation involving the issue of when work on a new office building will be completed, the owner demands that the project must be completed before the end of the year. This is a position, not an interest. To explore what the owner's underlying interest is, the contractor could ask, "Can you help me understand why that's important to you?" The owner's answer may be that the lease on his current

---

[23]   Roger Fisher, William Ury & Bruce Patton, GETTING TO YES: NEGOTIATING AGREEMENT WITHOUT GIVING IN (3rd ed,) at 50 (New York: Penguin Books, 2011).

[24]   Roger Fisher & Danny Ertel, GETTING READY TO NEGOTIATE at 22 (New York: Penguin Books, 1995).

building expires at the end of the year, and he would have to agree to an entire one-year extension if he cannot move into the new building by the first of the year. Once this interest is identified, the negotiation can be about paying for the cost of a move into temporary office space, or subsidizing the cost of a one-year lease extension on the current building (e.g., by means of a sublease), rather than about whether construction on the new building must be completed by the end of the year.

Interests also include avoiding or minimizing fears or concerns about things we do not like. For example, in plea-bargaining in a white-collar criminal case (which is a type of distributive negotiation), the defendant may wish to avoid incarceration completely, but that is not possible. Therefore, the negotiation with the prosecutor involves trying to satisfy the defendant's interests in limiting the amount of imprisonment to the shortest period possible and serving the sentence in a minimum security facility so as to avoid being housed with violent criminals.

4. GENERATING OPTIONS IN NEGOTIATION

In integrative negotiation, after the negotiators have identified the problem to be solved and have understood their respective important interests that must be satisfied, they can begin creating a list of options that are possible solutions of the problem. In this option-generation phase, the negotiators imagine or invent as many solutions as possible before they begin to critique or reject any of them. In using this kind of brainstorming, the options do not have to be acceptable or even feasible, e.g., some aspect of an otherwise unworkable option may ultimately be included as part of a mutually acceptable agreement.

In the example above, about the seller who demands payment in cash, her underlying interest (i.e., she wants certainty that she will be fully paid) can be used by the buyer to generate options (i.e., the ways in which the seller's interest might be satisfied). Because the seller wants to ensure she is paid in full, it may turn out that she is willing to accept a cashier's check or an electronic funds transfer into her bank account rather than payment of cash. She also may be willing to give the buyer a discount off the sales price if she is paid immediately in cash. She may be willing to accept payments over time, if the buyer takes delivery of the item being purchased only when full payment has been made. Or she may be willing to accept payments over time, if the buyer makes a substantial down-payment, agrees to pay a market rate of interest on the balance, executes a well-drafted promissory note, and signs a security agreement that the seller can publicly record for the item being purchased. These are all options that might satisfy her interest in ensuring she is fully paid.

Options are, in effect, answers to contingent "if" or "what-if" questions such as: "If we were to do X, would that satisfy your concern?" or "What if we were to do Y?" Options also can be problem-solving tactics or creative strategies for satisfying important interests. For example:

- One option might require one or both negotiators to unpack a complex interest into two or more sub-interests that can be addressed separately (e.g., the negotiators may disagree on the total amount of "damages" that were incurred, but can agree that "out-of-pocket expenses" should be paid now).

- Another option might require one negotiator to pay the other negotiator a sum of money to accept a specific solution, e.g., "I'll pay you $X, but only if you agree to dismiss your lawsuit with prejudice."

- Another option might require the negotiators to obtain additional resources to make the option feasible, e.g., both agree to sign on a bank loan so that one business partner can cash out the other partner now and repay the loan over time.

- Another option might require one or both negotiators to give away or give up certain interests to make an option acceptable, e.g., "I'll pay you $X as a signing bonus, if you accept my salary offer."

- Another option might require each negotiator to trade an important interest, e.g., "I'll give you X, if you give me Y."

- Another option might require each negotiator to dilute an interest so that each negotiator gets "half a loaf," e.g., "I'll give you half of X, if you give me two-thirds of Y."

- Another option may be to redefine the problem and agree to solve a different problem than the one the negotiators initially addressed, e.g., the problem is not how to pay the seller in cash, but rather is how to ensure that the seller has no risk of economic loss.

5.   EVALUATING OPTIONS USING OBJECTIVE CRITERIA OF LEGITIMACY

The next stage in negotiation is to evaluate options and select one to implement as the parties' agreement. This phase requires the negotiators to employ a decision-making process to weigh and rank in order the options and then select an option in terms of acceptability and satisfaction. To be selected, an option must be workable, meet my interests well, and at least meet your interests acceptably.[25]

One decision-making process is to agree to the selection criteria before evaluating the options. For example, if the problem to be solved is to select a candidate for a new job, the negotiators can agree first to a specific job description, including the duties the incumbent must perform and the experience and education the incumbent must possess. Once the

---

[25] The Harvard Negotiation Project has identified these criteria as a definition of an acceptable option.

negotiators have agreed to the job description, they can use the criteria contained in the job description to objectively evaluate the various candidates independently of the negotiators' personal preferences about particular candidates.

In evaluating options, negotiators should be alert for the following issues:[26]

> A negotiator may become defensive if asked to justify a personal preference. A "why" question (such as "Why do you like that option?") challenges a negotiator to justify himself in terms of his perception of his identity or personal values, which can feel threatening to him.

> A negotiator may prefer a specific option because of some undisclosed, indirect interest which the option satisfies, e.g., the negotiator may get significant approval from his client or get an economic bonus for achieving this particular solution.

> If a large group has been struggling with the solution of a large, complex problem, a small working group may be more productive in evaluating options and recommending one for approval by the members of the large group.

> It is not unusual for strained emotions to surface (or resurface) late in the option-evaluation phase because negotiators are in effect being asked to give up or compromise some interest to obtain a mutually acceptable solution. These late-emerging negative emotions must be managed effectively to avoid impasse.

> To obtain a mutually acceptable solution, it is possible to unpack complex options into subparts that can be exchanged or relinquished. It also is possible to combine parts of several different options into a new package that is more workable, satisfying, or objectively fair.

> Because of (disclosed or undisclosed) differences in risk aversion, or differences in expectations about future conditions, or differences in timing preferences, one party may be able to demand more (or the other party may be willing to accept less) than would otherwise seem objectively fair under the circumstances to an outside observer.

6. ASSESSING ALTERNATIVES IN NEGOTIATION

In any negotiation, a negotiator should agree to an offer only if it is better than his BATNA. If the offer is worse than his BATNA, the negotiator should not accept the offer and should pursue the BATNA instead.

In market-based distributive negotiation (e.g., buying and selling a used car), the negotiators' respective BATNAs determine their stopping points in the negotiation which, in turn, often are determined by relevant legit-

---

[26] See generally Roy J. Lewicki, Joseph A. Litterer, John W. Minton & David M. Saunders, NEGOTIATION (2nd ed.) at 97–100 (Illinois: Irwin, 1994).

imacy information. For example, the prospective seller and purchaser of a used car each do online research where they learn that a used car of this age, mileage, and condition sells locally in a range between $4X and $6X. The seller's BATNA should be to walk away from any offer below $4X, because there are other buyers in the market who are willing to pay at least $4X. The buyer's BATNA should be to walk away from any demand above $6X, because there are other sellers in the market who are willing to sell such a car for $6X.

In plea-bargaining distributive negotiation in a criminal case, the negotiators' respective BATNAs determine their stopping points in the negotiation. The negotiators' BATNAs may be determined by policy, precedent, or need. For example, the prosecutor in a tax fraud case may be constrained by policy from accepting an Alford plea from the defendant (i.e., a plea in which the defendant denies guilt but accepts that there is sufficient evidence to convict him beyond a reasonable doubt at trial). The prosecutor in a multi-count serious felony case may be permitted by precedents to accept a plea to one count of the lowest level of felony that is charged. In a multi-defendant felony case in which the prosecutor needs a defendant's testimony at trial to convict the co-defendant, the defendant may demand to make a plea to a misdemeanor or else the defendant will not agree to testify at trial.

In civil litigation, it often is necessary to conduct risk analysis (e.g., of the probability of an adverse result at trial, or the likely amount of the award of damages by a jury). To conduct realistic risk analysis is very challenging because a negotiator in litigation tends to look at the evidence through the perspective of her client (this is the so-called "advocate's bias"), even if she also tries to see the evidence from her opponent's point of view. Therefore, she should be aware that her advocate's bias can inflate her perception of the strength of her BATNA (i.e., she believes it is stronger than it actually is) and also can diminish her perception of the weakness of her opponent's BATNA (i.e., she believes it is weaker than it actually is). This phenomenon of the advocate's bias is seen often by mediators in litigated disputes, where the mediated settlement is less than the plaintiff's initial valuation of the case and greater than the defendant's initial valuation.

7.   MAKING COMMITMENTS IN NEGOTIATION

A commitment in negotiation may be tactical, e.g., a negotiator may demand some pre-agreement concession or else threaten to end the negotiation: "I will negotiate with you, if you give me X." The implied threat is that, if you do not first give him X, he will not negotiate with you.

A take-it-or-leave-it demand is an attempt at a strategic commitment that often creates resentment on the part of the other negotiator and can cause a negotiation to deadlock. Such a demand can be accepted if it is reasonable, or it can be ignored, or it can be rejected and met with a counteroffer. Take-it-or-leave-it demands often are made when a negotiator is angry or frustrated, so it is important to attend carefully to the negotiating relationship and the quality of communication during a negotiation. In making such a demand, if the negotiator appears to be bluffing about the take-it-or-leave-it demand, the other negotiator can disclose relevant legitimacy information or discuss the relative weakness of the demander's BATNA.

It is not unusual for disputes to arise when parties attempt to reduce the deal terms of their "handshake" agreement to writing or when negotiators attempt to obtain formal approval of the deal terms from their absent principals. Negotiators should not be surprised by and must be willing to negotiate these late-emerging differences.

While reaching a tentative final agreement, the negotiators should consider other strategic commitment issues such as:

- Are all issues of interest to the parties addressed?
- Is the agreement reasonably fair to both parties?
- Does the agreement *in total* make sense?
- Have all parties affected by the agreement been consulted? Do they agree?
- Do the parties have formal authority to enter into the agreement? Must others take action?
- Have the parties specified in detail what is to be done, by whom, by what time, how, and pursuant to what standards?
- Are the parties likely to perform future conditions? Is risk anticipated? Is it allocated?
- Does the agreement involve future payments? Are interest rate, default, and security terms necessary? Have they been agreed to?

C. THE SEVEN ELEMENTS IN THE FOUR NEGOTIATION STRATEGIES

Each of the four negotiation strategies has a unique goal, which affects the relative importance of the Seven Elements:

- in performative negotiation, the goal is to improve the parties' communication;
- in transformative negotiation, the goal is to improve the parties' relationship;
- in integrative negotiation, the goal is creative problem-solving; and
- in distributive negotiation, the goal is a fair exchange of value.

Given these four different goals, the Seven Elements manifest themselves differently in the four negotiation strategies.

1. THE SEVEN ELEMENTS IN PERFORMATIVE NEGOTIATION

I.   In performative negotiation, the negotiators' **relationship** often is polarized or adversarial, or at least reflects the negotiators' suspicions of one another.

II.   Because the goal of performative negotiation is to improve the negotiators' **communication**, this particular element is the most important of the seven. The negotiators' communication may involve telling and repeating conflict stories or stating and repeating demands or positions. In performative negotiation, the negotiators engage in very little effective listening, because they usually are not interested in understanding one another's perspectives. They also may engage in manipulation or deception, seeking to intimidate the other to give up his conflict story or forego his position. If the negotiators' communication improves, their negotiating relationship may improve as well.

III.   The negotiators each have their respective **interests** which they usually do not directly disclose in performative negotiation. Their apparent, observable interest is trying to persuade the other that their conflict story or demand is correct and, therefore, should be accepted by the other.

IV.   The negotiators' **options** in performative negotiation are either to continue to repeat their respective conflict stories or positions, or else to engage in what will be a difficult conversation by giving and taking turns listening and speaking.

V.   In performative negotiation, **legitimacy** information about precedents or objective standards of fairness is not particularly relevant, because the negotiators are not trying to persuade one another based on reason. Both sides believe that the legitimacy of their positions is self-evident and compelling.

VI.   The negotiators' **alternatives** in performative negotiation often are weak or unacceptable, which is why they are negotiating with each other. Because their walk-away alternative is not feasible, they often exaggerate or misrepresent their BATNAs, seeking to bluff or deceive one another through doubt-creating behaviors.

VII.   In performative negotiation, the negotiators' **commitment** is reflected in their joint (though perhaps temporary) participation in the negotiation process. Because they are locked into exchanging verbal volleys of conflict stories or positions, they cannot engage in productive negotiation that leads to a mutually acceptable agreement.

2. THE SEVEN ELEMENTS IN TRANSFORMATIVE NEGOTIATION

I.   Because the goal of transformative negotiation is to improve the negotiators' **relationship**, this particular element is the most important of the seven. In transformative negotiation, the negotiators' relationship often is strained and may even be polarized or adversarial. Therefore, the goal of transformative negotiation is to repair a damaged relationship or replace it with a new and different kind of relationship.

II. The negotiators' **communication** involves controlling the expression of negative emotions, giving and taking turns, respectfully listening and responsively speaking, and seeking to understand one another's perspectives, both factually and emotionally. This requires "active listening" which includes: listening without interrupting; listening to feelings as well as to content; using attending and prompting behaviors to incentivize the other negotiator to keep talking; and using reflection and summarizing to demonstrate that the listener comprehends what the other negotiator is saying, both emotionally and factually. As the negotiators' communication improves, their relationship improves, as well.

III. The negotiators' **interests** in transformative negotiation are to improve or change their relationship. An important interest may include making an apology by recognizing that one has harmed the other, acknowledging the harm, committing not to repeat the harm, and making amends. Accepting a sincere apology and moving on may be an important interest, too.

IV. The negotiators' **options** in transformative negotiation are the various ways in which the negotiators can work together to improve or change their relationship.

V.   In transformative negotiation, **legitimacy** may include information about how people in other effective or successful relationships treat one another. It may also include information about how people in similar stressed relationships have worked together to improve or change those relationships.

VI. The negotiators' **alternatives** in transformative negotiation often are weak or unacceptable. For example, it may not be possible for a negotiator to terminate the relationship, and it may not be possible for a negotiator to maintain the status quo of a stressed relationship.

VII. In transformative negotiation, the negotiators' **commitment** is reflected in their ongoing willingness to undertake efforts to improve or change their relationship.

3. THE SEVEN ELEMENTS IN INTEGRATIVE NEGOTIATION

I. Because the goal of integrative negotiation is to work together to create a deal or resolve a problem in a mutually acceptable manner, the effectiveness of the negotiators' negotiating **relationship** is important. Furthermore, the negotiators (or at least their respective clients) may have had a past relationship or may need to create an ongoing future relationship.

II. The negotiators' **communication** in integrative negotiation often involves sharing information about important interests and about ways in which those interests might be met in a negotiated agreement. Effective communication skills in integrative negotiation include active listening, perspective-taking, and assertiveness.

III. The negotiators' **interests** in integrative negotiation are to satisfy their respective needs and wants to the fullest extent possible.

IV. The negotiators' **options** in integrative negotiation are the various ways in which the negotiators can work together to create a deal or resolve a problem in a mutually acceptable manner. Negotiators often generate multiple options by focusing on their underlying interests. Integrative options also typically seek to increase the amount of "pie" available to be allocated between the negotiators.

V. In integrative negotiation, **legitimacy** may include information about how people in similar situations have worked together to create a deal or resolve a problem. As with distributive negotiation (discussed below), it is also common for integrative negotiators to look to objective standards to provide legitimacy.

VI. The negotiators' **alternatives** in integrative negotiation often are to walk away without agreeing to an unacceptable offer or demand.

VII. In integrative negotiation, the negotiators' **commitment** is reflected in their efforts to fulfill the deal terms of their negotiated agreement, which often is written and signed by the negotiators (or their principals) as a binding, enforceable contract.

4. THE SEVEN ELEMENTS IN DISTRIBUTIVE NEGOTIATION

I. Distributive negotiation is characteristic of market-based bargaining (e.g., the buying and selling of a used car). Because the

goal of distributive negotiation is to exchange value in an acceptable manner, the effectiveness of the negotiators' negotiating
relationship is not as important as the elements of legitimacy
and alternatives.

II. The negotiators' **communication** in distributive negotiation
often is less personable and more business-like than in
integrative negotiation. Their communication may involve
bluffing about the actual strength of their alternatives or puffing
their opinions about value. Usually in distributive negotiation
the negotiators do not candidly and completely disclose details
about their underlying important interests. Effective
communication in distributive negotiation often is calculated to
express the appearance of good preparation, assertiveness, and
confidence.

III. The negotiators in distributive negotiation generally do not
mutually explore their underlying **interests**, which they often
intentionally conceal from one another. In essence, distributive
negotiation is a zero-sum game in which the size of the
negotiating pie is fixed, and the negotiators are dividing it
between them. In market-based distributive negotiation, the
seller's apparent interest is in getting the highest price possible,
whereas the buyer's apparent interest is in paying the lowest
price possible. In plea-bargaining, which is another form of
distributive negotiation, the most favorable outcome for the
defendant is to reduce the amount of a fine or the period of
incarceration, i.e., the defendant's interest is to achieve the least
unfavorable outcome under the circumstances.

IV. The negotiators' **options** in distributive negotiation are limited
because the parties are not mutually exploring their underlying
interests. Therefore, the negotiators' options are the offers and
counteroffers exchanged in the bargaining process. The opening
offer and counteroffer in distributive negotiation usually are aggressive, either for the purpose of trying to anchor the other's
expectation about the ultimate settlement value, or testing the
degree of the other's lack of preparation and inexperience. In
market-based distributive negotiation, the seller typically starts
with a high sales price, and the buyer counters with a low pur-
chase price. The exchange of offers and counteroffers funnels the
gap between the negotiators' opening positions into a zone of
possible agreement.

V. In distributive negotiation, **legitimacy** often includes objective
standards of value such as appraisals or comparable sales prices.
Legitimacy is one of the two most important elements in distributive negotiation.

VI. The other important structural element in distributive negotiation is the relative strength or weakness of the negotiators' **alternatives**. Negotiators who have strong alternatives in distributive negotiation are ready, willing, and able to walk away without agreeing to an unacceptable demand. A strong alternative is one of the most effective tools that a distributive negotiator can use to leverage the most favorable outcome under the circumstances, e.g., if the buyer can buy a similar car at a lower price from another seller down the street, the buyer has a strong alternative and should be able to leverage significant movement from the seller in the current negotiation.

VII. In distributive negotiation, the negotiators' **commitment** is reflected in their exchange of value (e.g., the payment of cash for a car in exchange for its possession and title). Agreements that require future payments or future performance pose unique challenges that often are addressed as contingencies in a well-written, binding, enforceable contract signed by the negotiators (or their clients).

Effective negotiators are able to appropriately and flexibly employ all four kinds of negotiation principles as needed to achieve the outcomes they desire. As negotiators increasingly understand when and how to use four different sets of negotiation concepts and skills systematically, they have more powerful tools to wield in creating deals and settling disputes.

EXERCISE

Identifying the Seven Elements of Negotiation

Analyze a negotiation in which you participated and identify as many of the Seven Elements as you can that were involved in the negotiation.

* * *

Analyzing Your Childhood Experience of Conflict Communication

"The people whose behaviors we find most difficult to handle may conduct themselves in ways reminiscent of the parent with whom we have not fully resolved our differences. Often, they are people who developed patterns of compensating behavior exactly opposite to ours, or who engage in behaviors we had to struggle to overcome, or who simply remind us of the difficulties we had as children in getting our needs met."[27]

Answer the following three questions:

- When you were a child, how did your family handle conflicts within the family?

---

[27] Kenneth Cloke & Joan Goldsmith, RESOLVING CONFLICTS AT WORK 180 (San Francisco: Jossey–Bass Publishers, 2000).

- If you had a conflict with a parent or a sibling, how were you required to act and speak?

- Do you see any similarities or differences with how you handle conflict now?

People who have analyzed their childhood experience of conflict communication typically report either that they handle conflict similarly now as adults, or they have chosen as adults to handle conflict very differently.

EXERCISE

The Jockey Negotiation[28]

Using the Seven Elements of Negotiation to Represent Calomite Stables

The following exercise is a negotiation between the representative of Calomite Stables and the representative of jockey Cristo Lines. Confidential information for Calomite Stables's representative is on the following page. Confidential information for Cristo Lines' representative is on the second page following this one. Both parties should read the following general information:

General Information

Calomite Stables has lost its regular jockey who was scheduled to ride Calomite's outstanding three-year-old thoroughbred racehorse, Flashdance, in the Kentucky Derby next week. Cristo Lines is a young and upcoming jockey who has never ridden in a Triple Crown race (i.e., the Kentucky Derby, the Preakness, or the Belmont). Cristo is the only experienced racing jockey available on such short notice and Calomite wants to negotiate with Cristo's agent about riding Flashdance. A top jockey can earn $45,000 for riding in all three Triple Crown races.

---

[28] See generally "Negotiation in the Practice of Law: A Video Companion" (Philadelphia: American Law Institute–American Bar Association).

Confidential Information for Calomite's Representative

Calomite wants to sign Cristo to ride Flashdance. Calomite was going to pay its regular jockey $15,000 to ride Flashdance in just the Kentucky Derby. Calomite's exercise jockey (who has never ridden in a big race) could ride Flashdance, for which Calomite would pay her $5,000. Calomite is willing to pay Cristo up to $20,000 to ride Flashdance in the Derby.

Instructions for Calomite's Representative

- In representing Calomite Stables, use the Seven Elements of negotiation to prepare to negotiate with Cristo Lines' representative:

- What kind of negotiation **relationship** do you want to have with Cristo's representative?

- What style of **communication** do you want to use with Cristo's representative?

- What are Calomite's and Cristo's **interests** in negotiating with one another?

- What are some **options** that might satisfy the interests of both parties?

- What is some **legitimacy** information you may want to disclose to Cristo's representative and what is some legitimacy information you may want to obtain?

- What is Calomite's best **alternative**, if you cannot reach agreement?

- What kind of **commitment** can you make to Cristo, and what kind of commitment do you want Cristo to make to Calomite? How will these commitments be memorialized?

What are you going to say to start the negotiation? At what point will you stop negotiating? Why?

Confidential Information for Cristo Lines' Representative

Cristo usually gets paid $2,500 to $5,000 per race. Once, last year, he earned $10,000 to ride in the Oaks. He would ride Flashdance for free just to get the exposure and experience of riding a contender in the Kentucky Derby from a major stable like Calomite Stables.

Instructions for Cristo Lines' Representative

In representing Cristo Lines, use the Seven Elements of negotiation to prepare to negotiate with Calomite Stables' representative:

- What kind of negotiation **relationship** do you want to have with Calomite's representative?

- What style of **communication** do you want to use with Calomite's representative?

- What are Cristo's and Calomite's **interests** in negotiating with one another?

- What are some **options** that might satisfy the interests of both parties?

- What is some **legitimacy** information you may want to disclose to Calomite's representative and what is some legitimacy information you may want to obtain?

- What is Christo's best **alternative**, if you cannot reach agreement?

- What kind of **commitment** can you make to Calomite, and what kind of commitment do you want Calomite to make to Cristo? How will these commitments be memorialized?

What are you going to say to start the negotiation? At what point will you stop negotiating? Why?

CHAPTER 2

NEGOTIATION AND MEDIATION STYLES

■ ■ ■

In this book we use "style" to refer to a person's manner of expression using verbal and non-verbal communicative behaviors. We use "strategy" to refer to a plan incorporating specific principles (concepts and skills) designed to achieve an intended outcome. Adjectives like "collaborative" are synonyms of a cooperative style, whereas adjectives like "aggressive" are synonyms of a competitive style. In terms of style, negotiators can be cooperative or competitive. By contrast, in terms of strategy, negotiations and mediations have one or more of four kinds of intended outcomes, including:

1) improving the quality of the communication between negotiators or parties ("performative negotiation");

2) creating or changing the relationship between negotiators or parties ("transformative negotiation");

3) creatively solving a shared problem between negotiators or parties ("integrative negotiation"); and

4) fairly exchanging value between negotiators or parties ("distributive negotiation").

A. NEGOTIATION STYLES

Negotiators employing a performative strategy or a distributive strategy often express these strategies using a competitive style. Negotiators employing a transformative strategy or an integrative strategy often express these strategies using a cooperative style. However, we also can counter-intuitively describe a negotiator as employing a distributive strategy but using a cooperative style, or as employing an integrative strategy but using a competitive style.

Our purpose here is to help negotiators become more self-aware of the existence of two styles of negotiating (cooperative and competitive) and four strategies of negotiating (performative, transformative, integrative, and distributive). The self-aware negotiator thereby can choose which negotiating style and strategy to use first in a specific negotiation, and also can choose to change or modify the negotiating style or strategy in order to achieve more effectively the intended outcome of the negotiation.

We turn now to an analysis of the research and related conclusions about two kinds of negotiators, which are contained in one of the first seminal books on legal negotiation. We believe the book conflates style and strategy. However, its research-based observations provide important concrete descriptions of cooperative versus competitive negotiating styles, together with credible explanations of why a cooperative style often is more effective in legal negotiation than a competitive style.

1. GERALD WILLIAMS' STUDIES OF COOPERATIVE AND COMPETITIVE NEGOTIATORS[1]

Professor Gerald R. Williams and others conducted research in the 1970s of the effectiveness of lawyers as negotiators, the results of which he reported in his 1983 book, LEGAL NEGOTIATION AND SETTLEMENT. The research included lawyers' answers to questionnaires, audiotaped interviews and self-reports of lawyer-negotiators, and videotaped recordings of experienced lawyers engaged in negotiating legal disputes and business transactions. The results showed that most lawyers (65%) used a cooperative approach to negotiation and a smaller number (24%) used a competitive approach, with the remaining 11% of lawyers who did not identify using either approach.

Williams' research also showed that 49% of lawyers were rated by their peers as "effective" negotiators, 38% were rated as "average" negotiators, and 12% were rated as "ineffective" negotiators. The vast majority of cooperative lawyer-negotiators were rated as effective or average. Competitive lawyer-negotiators were about evenly distributed among effective, average, and ineffective. These findings are summarized in the following table:

Degree of Effectiveness	Cooperative Approach	Competitive Approach
Effective Negotiators (49% of the Bar)	38%	6%
Average Negotiators (38% of the Bar)	24%	10%
Ineffective Negotiators (12% of the Bar)	2%	8%
Total (99% of the Bar)	Total (65% of the Bar)*	Total (24% of the Bar)*

   * 11% of the Bar did not identify using either a cooperative or competitive approach.

---

[1]   See generally Gerald R. Williams, LEGAL NEGOTIATION AND SETTLEMENT (St. Paul, MN: West Publishing Co., 1983).

According to Williams' research, effective cooperative negotiators act ethically, are concerned about fairness, and want to establish and maintain a good working relationship with the other negotiator. They accurately estimate the value of their case, know their client's needs, take a realistic opening position, and probe the other side's position. They are willing to share information and willing to move from their opening position. They are courteous, personable, friendly, tactful, sincere, forthright, trustworthy, objective, fair-minded, and reasonable. They do not use threats and they are well-organized, wise, and careful.

By contrast, effective competitive negotiators are concerned about maximizing their own interests and those of their client. They are ambitious, arrogant, egotistical, clever, and rigid. They act tough, dominantly, forcefully, and aggressively. They make unrealistically high (or low) opening demands, are willing to stretch the facts, reveal information gradually, and are careful about the timing and sequence of moves. They obstruct and use threats. They do not consider the needs of the other side and they are not concerned about their relationship with the other negotiator or the other client.

Effective cooperative negotiators and effective competitive negotiators share a number of characteristics. They are both seen as being experienced, realistic, ethical, rational, trustworthy, convincing, analytical, creative, self-controlled, versatile, adaptable, poised, legally astute, honest, professional, intelligent, thoroughly prepared, perceptive, and engaged.

Williams' research revealed that ineffective cooperative negotiators do not have the experience or skills to be perceptive, convincing, realistic, rational, analytical, creative, self-controlled, versatile, adaptable, objective, and legally astute. They lack confidence and are unsure of the value of their case.

Ineffective competitive negotiators are headstrong, impatient, intolerant, rigid, loud, greedy, demanding, unreasonable, obnoxious, arrogant, tactless, complaining, sarcastic, insincere, devious, conniving, impulsive, unpredictable, evasive, suspicious, distrustful, unskilled at reading others' cues, rude, hostile, and obstructive. They also were unsure of the value of their case, took unrealistic opening positions, did not move from their opening positions, used take-it-or-leave-it tactics, were unwilling to share information, used bluffs and threats, and were disinterested in the other negotiator and the other client.

According to Williams, there are many more effective cooperative negotiators than effective competitive negotiators. He concludes that there may be little choice involved in whether one is a cooperative or competitive negotiator, because one's basic approach to negotiation is determined largely by personality and experience. However, he believes that negotiators can shift from one approach to another and are more likely to be cooperative in some circumstances and competitive in others. This kind of versatility is important for lawyers because their professional obligation (as agents) is to effectively represent the interests of their clients (as principals).

Williams contends that competitive negotiators use psychological tactics to adversely affect the emotions of other negotiators. They have high aspirations about outcomes; they make high demands and few concessions; and they use exaggeration, bluffs, threats, ridicule, and accusations to put pressure on their opponents. They use tactics of manipulation and deception to cause their opponents to lose confidence in themselves and the merits of their cases, to reduce their opponents' expectations of what they can achieve as outcomes, and to induce their opponents to accept less than they otherwise would have obtained on the merits.

Williams' research revealed that tactics of manipulation and deception have limitations that reduce their effectiveness. These tactics provoke reciprocal responses, increase tension and mistrust, distort communications between negotiators, generate misunderstandings, create impasses that end negotiations, damage long-term relationships, and impair the reputations of competitive negotiators. Opponents also are offended by competitive negotiators' unfair treatment and opponents retaliate by working harder to create obstacles and increase costs. In addition, threats are improper and legally actionable if what is threatened is a crime (such as use of physical violence), a tort (such as wrongful seizure of property or intentional interference with contractual rights), initiation of criminal prosecution, or bad-faith use of civil process. Similarly, fraudulent deception and intentional material factually relevant misrepresentation in negotiation are improper and actionable.

Cooperative negotiators use psychological tactics to positively affect the emotions of other negotiators. They seek a common ground of shared interests, values, and attitudes; they use rational persuasion and unilateral concessions to incentivize reciprocal cooperative responses; they promote trust by appearing not to seek unfair advantage for themselves or their clients; and their goal in negotiations is to obtain an objectively fair outcome using processes perceived by other negotiators as fair.

According to Williams' research, effective cooperative lawyer-negotiators settled 84% of their cases and went to trial on the remaining 16%, whereas effective competitive lawyer-negotiators settled two-thirds of their cases and went to trial on the remaining third.

Williams believes that ineffective cooperative negotiators fail to perceive competitive tactics, blindly continue to cooperate with competitive negotiators, continue to make unilateral concessions, and fail to obtain reciprocal value in return. Competitive negotiators perceive this as weakness and therefore increase their demands and expectations about what they can obtain.

Legal negotiations go through stages that begin with lawyers establishing their negotiating relationships, articulating their respective positions, arguing the strengths and merits of their positions, trying to discover others' real interests without disclosing their own, defining the issues to be negotiated, changing others' expectations about outcome, proposing new alternatives, making concessions, agreeing and formalizing agreement, or else reaching impasse and ending the negotiation.

An opening position can be "maximalist" and demand more than the negotiator expects to obtain, or can be "equitable" and ask for outcomes fair to both sides, or can be "integrative" by identifying and evaluating alternatives that maximize benefits to each side's interests (citing GETTING TO YES by Roger Fisher and William Ury). Williams believes that integrative bargaining is used by both effective cooperative and effective competitive negotiators.

In the first or opening-position stage of negotiation, each negotiator attempts to create the "illusion" of being inalterably committed to his opening position. The objective of this illusion is to give credibility to a high (or low) opening demand and thereby diminish the other negotiator's hopes or expectations about the value of the case or the ultimate outcome of the negotiation. Very little real negotiation occurs in this first stage.

Williams believes that in the second or "argumentation" stage of negotiation, each negotiator seeks to obtain information about the real expectations of the other negotiator without disclosing one's own minimal expectations. Whatever information is exchanged is presented in a way most favorable to the presenter. According to Williams, this argumentation stage helps define the issues to be negotiated and begins to make more apparent the strengths and weaknesses of each side. During the argumentation stage, a cooperative negotiator will begin making concessions, thereby seeking to create a trusting atmosphere and incentivize reciprocal responses of equal value. By contrast, a competitive negotiator will accept the other's concessions, while making few and small concessions in response.

The third stage of negotiation is one of "emergence and crisis" caused by an impending deadline, an unacceptable final offer, or an apparently unbridgeable gap between the negotiators' positions. At this point, the negotiator must decide whether to take the other's final offer, leave it, or do something else (e.g., continue to negotiate while preparing for trial).

The fourth stage of negotiation according to Williams is reaching agreement or final breakdown. If agreement is reached, the details must be worked out and reduced to writing, which often requires ongoing negotiation. Apparent breakdowns can be tactical rather than final (e.g., when a negotiator declares a breakdown only to pressure the other negotiator to make more movement or another concession).

DISCUSSION TOPICS

1. Are there more than two styles of negotiating (i.e., cooperative and competitive)?

2. Must a negotiator make an either/or choice between these two negotiation styles?

3. What happens when two competitive negotiators move psychologically against one another?

4. Is an effective cooperative negotiator at a disadvantage when negotiating with an effective competitive negotiator?

5. Can a cooperative negotiator influence a competitive negotiator to adopt a cooperative style of negotiating?

EXERCISE

Analyze an important negotiation in which you participated and identify what negotiation styles were used by the parties. How did these styles affect the interpersonal behavior of the negotiators? Did the negotiators' styles affect the outcome of the negotiation?

EXERCISE

Thumb–Wrestling Contest: Score as Much as You Can

The objective of this "thumb-wrestling" contest is for you to score as many points as you can in 15 seconds. Here are the rules of the competition (which you and a partner should read carefully before you start):

1. Choose a partner.

2. You cannot talk to your partner about the contest.

3. Hold the fingers of your partner's right hand with the fingers of your right hand; your thumb and your partner's thumb should be pointed straight up to start.

4. Have an observer give you and your partner the instruction, "Get set."

5. When the observer says, "Go," try to pin your partner's thumb with your thumb.

6. Each time you pin your partner's thumb, you get one point.

7. Keep track of your points by saying out loud, "One," "Two," and so on.

8. The observer will call "Stop" at the end of 15 seconds.

9. Write down how many points you scored: _____

10. Discuss the objective of the contest with your partner and then repeat the contest. Compare the points you scored during the first contest with those you scored in the second contest.

This exercise demonstrates the differing effect on outcomes of competitive versus cooperative approaches.

B. MEDIATION STYLES

Based on differences in personality, background, training, or experience, mediators adopt particular styles or techniques they deem appropriate to helping parties come to an agreement. These styles are generally classified in four ways: facilitative, analytical, evaluative, and directive. Mediators vary in their opinions of which mediation style is most conducive to resolving disputes. While some mediators may rely heavily on a particular style, often mediators employ one or more of the other styles at various stages within a mediation session.

1.   FACILITATIVE

The facilitative style is classical mediation in which the mediator helps the parties improve their ability to communicate and negotiate. Mediators using the facilitative style see their role as limited in terms of substance; the parties are responsible for the control of substance and outcome and the mediator merely facilitates discussion and negotiation. While facilitative mediators may exercise control of ground rules, they generally refrain from offering any substantive ideas regarding the outcome, preferring instead to elicit ideas from the parties. The underlying philosophy is that parties are more likely to create a durable agreement that is satisfactory to both parties if solutions come from the parties themselves rather than from the mediator.

Example: In a dispute between a private developer and a representative from an environmental group about the impact of a new housing development on a nearby river, a facilitative mediator might begin by explaining the ground rules for the mediation, give each side an opportunity to explain her perspective, and then ask questions that facilitate a discussion between the two parties. The mediator might ask the environmental representative, "You mentioned that you feel strongly about preserving the existing trees in the area. Can you explain to the developer why that's important to you?" Or to the developer, "You said that dealing with environmental groups is unproductive. Can you tell her more about why you feel that way?" By asking questions that explore each side's interests or concerns, the facilitative mediator would continue to assist the parties in engaging in a productive discussion.

2. ANALYTICAL

With the analytical style, the mediator asks questions of the parties or their counsel to help the parties analyze issues, options, and the risks of not resolving the dispute. Analytical mediators often have expertise in particular areas of law, which enables them to engage in the substance of disputes within their experience. While stopping short of providing their own evaluation and recommendations (see evaluative and directive mediation below), analytical mediators become involved in the substance of the dispute by actively asking questions and raising issues that direct the discussion and assist the parties in thinking through the issues and their consequences. Sometimes analytical mediators must ask risk-analysis questions in caucus because a party does not wish to give candid answers in the presence of the other party.

Example: A software development company has accused a competitor of violating one of its patents. An analytical mediator who has a background in the computer industry might ask questions to both parties about the nature of the product, how each side went about developing their products, how the products are similar, what the market for each product looks like, how profits have been (or will be) affected, how much time and money each side anticipates spending if they take the dispute to court, etc. Through these types of questions, the analytical mediator would attempt to guide the parties toward an agreement. Sometimes candid answers to these risk-analysis questions occur only in caucus.

3. EVALUATIVE

Mediators using the evaluative style give their own opinions to the parties about the value of the case or the likely outcome of the dispute if it is not resolved. Evaluative mediators have subject-matter expertise that relates to the disputed issues and they facilitate further analysis by the parties by providing an appraisal of each side's strengths and weaknesses. Similar to "early neutral evaluation," evaluative mediators are deeply engaged in the substance of the dispute. They can suggest options for settlement and sometimes exert pressure on parties to come to an agreement. The evaluative style tends to emphasize efficiency and pays less attention to underlying needs and interests. Often, mediators give their evaluations in caucus after the parties have reached an impasse in the mediation and both parties have requested the mediator to be evaluative.

Example: A construction company claims that a homeowner refuses to pay for the work the company has recently completed. An evaluative mediator with expertise in the construction industry might gather information from both parties and then explain to the parties the strengths and weaknesses in their positions. The mediator might tell the construction company that, while it completed the work on schedule, the homeowner seems to have strong evidence that the work was substandard, and that information could be very detrimental to the company in court. Conversely, the mediator might tell the homeowner that the cost of litigating the dispute is much greater than the remaining amount owed to the construction company. By providing an assessment of both sides' strengths and weaknesses and the risks and expense they face in going to court, the evaluative mediator can help motivate the parties to come to an agreement that reflects the merits of the case as he has evaluated it.

4. DIRECTIVE

In the directive approach, by whatever means, the mediator substantively works to persuade one or both parties to settle the dispute in a specific way. Similar to the evaluative style, directive mediators tend to focus on efficiency over the relationship of the parties, and may be outcome-driven. Directive mediators express opinions about the substance of the dispute, offer ideas for settlement, and often direct parties to come to a specific agreement. Because the mediator tends to be heavily involved in both process and outcome, the directive style is somewhat similar to non-binding arbitration. Often, mediators give their advice or direction in caucus after the parties have reached an impasse in the mediation and both parties have requested the mediator to be directive.

Example: In a custody dispute between two parents, a directive mediator might listen to both parties' arguments, decide on an outcome that, from her perspective, seems consistent with what a court would order, propose the outcome to the parties, and then actively work to convince the parties to agree to accept her proposal. She might use phrases such as, "This may not seem like the most ideal arrangement to either of you, but you need to be realistic. It's the best outcome you're going to get when you go to court."

EXERCISE

A Conflict Resolution Preference Self–Inventory

Part I: Rating Your Negotiation Behavior in Negotiation with Strangers

For each statement, when negotiating with a stranger, indicate *how much the statement is characteristic of you* on the following scale:

1. Strongly uncharacteristic of me

2. Moderately uncharacteristic of me

3. Mildly uncharacteristic of me

4. Neutral: I have no opinion about this

5. Mildly characteristic of me

6. Moderately characteristic of me

7. Strongly characteristic of me

1. _____ I am always sincere and trustworthy. I will not lie, for whatever reason

2. _____ I would never secretly read my opponent's negotiation notes.

3. _____ I don't care what people think of me. Getting what I want is more important.

4. _____ I am uncomfortable when things are ambiguous.

5. _____ I can lie effectively. I can maintain a poker face when I don't tell the truth.

6. _____ I am highly principled. I stand by my principles no matter what the cost.

7. _____ I am a patient person. I do not care how long it takes to reach agreement.

8. _____ I am a good judge of character. I can quickly spot when I am being lied to.

9. _____ I use my sense of humor as one of my biggest assets in negotiation.

10. _____ I have above-average empathy for the views and feelings of my opponent.

11. _____ I don't take conflict seriously. I can argue, but then put that aside quickly.

12. _____ I tend to hold grudges.

13. _____ Criticism usually doesn't bother me. People often disagree with me.

14. _____ I like to use power to get what I want. I don't like to share power.

15. _____ I like to share power. Shared power results in better decision making.

16. _____ I don't like trying to persuade my opponent to my point of view.

17. _____ The best way to resolve differences is by arguing.

18. _____ I hate conflict and will do anything to avoid it.

19. _____ I like to win. Not just win, but win by the biggest margin possible.

20. _____ I negotiate by being completely honest with my opponent.

Part II: Rating a Stranger's Negotiation Behavior

For each statement, when negotiating with a stranger, indicate *how much you agree with the statement* on the following scale:

1. Strongly disagree
2. Moderately disagree
3. Mildly disagree
4. Neutral: I have no opinion about this
5. Mildly agree
6. Moderately agree
7. Strongly agree

21. _____ If you are too honest and trustworthy, people will take advantage of that.

22. _____ Fear is a stronger persuader than trust.

23. _____ If you are easily predictable, you are easily manipulated.

24. _____ If you make a concession, your opponent may later give you something.

25. _____ Your personality and ability to read people are more important than your knowledge of your opponent's interests and concerns.

26. _____ Silence is the best way to respond to an unacceptable offer.

27. _____ You must be aggressive if you are going to accomplish your objectives.

28. _____ Honesty and openness are necessary to reach fair agreements.

29. _____ Never lose your temper. Keeping your cool gives you an advantage.

30. _____ Keep a poker face. Never act pleased when you get what you want.

31. _____ To be effective, you must see the issues from your opponent's point of view.

32. _____ An unanswered threat will be seen as weakness. You must respond.

33. _____ In negotiation, winning is the most important consideration.

34. _____ The best outcome in negotiation is one which is fair to all parties.

35. _____ Most results in negotiation can be achieved through cooperation.

36. _____ Principles are good, but sometimes must be compromised to achieve goals.

37. _____ You should never exploit your opponent's personal weaknesses.

38. _____ Good ends justify the means. If you know you are right and your goal is worthy, you should not be concerned about how your goal is achieved.

39. _____ Making your opponent uncomfortable is okay if you win.

40. _____ There is nothing wrong with exaggerating so long as you are not lying.

Circle the 7s and the 1s in the 40 statements above. If there are few 7s and 1s, then also circle the 6s and the 2s. By analyzing the circled statements, try to identify a pattern that shows your preferences for conflict resolution when negotiating with a stranger. Put an X in the following chart that most accurately reflects your personal preferences for conflict resolution when negotiating with a stranger (you may have a different preference when negotiating with a friend or family member).

Transformative Negotiation

The relationship is the issue.

Integrative Negotiation

Creative deal making is the issue.

Performative Negotiation

Effective communication is the issue.

Distributive Negotiation

Fair exchange of value is the issue.

Parties' Concern for their Relationship

Low ← → Parties' Concern for Mutually Acceptable Outcome ← →

CHAPTER 3

USING THE FOUR STRATEGIES IN NEGOTIATION AND MEDIATION

■ ■ ■

As discussed previously, in terms of strategy, negotiations and mediations have one or more of four kinds of intended outcomes:

1) improving the quality of the communication between negotiators or parties ("performative negotiation");

2) creating or changing the relationship between negotiators or parties ("transformative negotiation");

3) creatively solving a shared problem between negotiators or parties ("integrative negotiation"); and

4) fairly exchanging value between negotiators or parties ("distributive negotiation").

This chapter will discuss the performative, transformative, integrative, and distributive strategies and how each relates to negotiation and mediation. Following a discussion of each strategy there is a section on skills or "tools" relevant to the strategies. Each section concludes with exercises designed to facilitate discussion and provide opportunities to put the concepts and skills into action.

A. PERFORMATIVE PRINCIPLES

There are two common performative conflict communication situations, both of which involve what in essence are repeated monologues. The first involves high-conflict communication in which the parties tell and repeat conflict stories that focus on the past and blame the other party as the wrongdoer, with no recognition of the speaker's contribution to the conflict. The second situation involves positional bargaining in which the parties state and repeat their positions, with little or no willingness to listen to one another. The challenge in both situations is for the parties to engage in conversation in which they are listening and communicating productively.

1. IN NEGOTIATION

For many, the performative approach to negotiation is a default strategy. One party approaches another with her conflict story, and the other reacts in-kind with his. In these situations, performative negotiation is often a very low-skill (or, arguably, no-skill) approach, characterized more by emotional—typically angry—responses that escalate, with each side listening only enough to take offense.

In its positional bargaining form, performative negotiation may consist of tactics such as manipulation, deception, or intimidation in an attempt to gain advantage. Parties haggle stubbornly, each insistent on her initial position, which is often extreme and unreasonable. Because each side has already firmly staked out her position, talking only seems to further entrench the parties.

Parties engaged solely in performative negotiation rarely come to an agreement. Caught in an unproductive, downward spiral, the parties usually stop talking after coming to a stalemate. Occasionally a party may surrender and yield to the other side's demands, but the agreement is then one-sided and often lacking in durability.

2. IN MEDIATION

The core purpose of performative mediation is for the mediator to help the parties convert their respective performative monologues (whether telling conflict stories or repeating their positional demands) into dialogue, i.e., to help them engage in conversation. To do this, the mediator conducts a structured process in which he:

- establishes ground rules (e.g., everyone must use first names, the parties will take turns talking and listening, the parties cannot interrupt each other's remarks, the parties must direct their comments to each other rather than to the mediator, etc.);
- gives each party an uninterrupted opportunity to tell her conflict story or state her position;
- intervenes to enforce the ground rules;
- asks questions that require first-person, present-tense answers;
- summarizes what he has heard the parties say, using their key words and reflecting their feelings;
- explains to the parties the importance of shifting the time frame of their remarks from past to present (because problem-solving can only occur in the present, not in the past); and
- asks the parties to talk to one another about what they want to do next.

Parties need to know they have been heard and understood. When a party feels her conflict story or positional demand has been acknowledged by the mediator, even though not agreed to by the other party, she often becomes willing to listen and begin engaging in a dialogue (which is a series of responsive turns in a conversation) with the other party. This conversational communication is necessary for the parties to begin problem-solving.

Mediation of legal disputes often begins performatively with the parties telling conflict stories or repeating positional demands. However, once the parties get past their monologues and begin to listen and talk to one another, the mediation typically slips almost seamlessly into transformative, integrative, or distributive mediation in which the mediator helps the parties engage in conversation about whatever is affecting their relationship or hindering their willingness to work together to resolve their mutual problem.

3. PERFORMATIVE SKILLS

The following are tools or skills that can be developed and employed in any negotiation or mediation, but tend to be especially relevant to the performative approach, given its high-conflict and emotional communication context.

The Toolbox:

- Awareness
    - Ladder of Inference
    - Ladder of Accusation
- Johari Windows
- Dealing with Emotions: Five Core Concerns
- Asking Questions
- Effective Listening
- Reframing

a. Awareness

During a performative negotiation or mediation, parties are so caught up in their personal conflict narrative that it is difficult for them to see anything beyond their own perspectives. They have reached a conclusion and, from their vantage point, it is the only reasonable and logical conclusion available. To help oneself or another party move beyond the performative stage, it is necessary for a party to broaden his (or the other party's) awareness.

Research confirms that negotiators with a higher perspective-taking ability negotiate agreements of higher value than those with lower perspective-taking ability.[1] However, research also has shown that negotiators routinely jump to mistaken conclusions about their

---

[1] See generally Robert H. Mnookin, Scott R. Peppet & Andrew S. Tulumello, BEYOND WINNING: NEGOTIATING TO CREATE VALUE IN DEALS AND DISPUTES 46–49 (Cambridge: Belnap Press of Harvard University Press, 2000).

counterparts' motivations, usually because their information is limited and they don't seek to acquire more information.[2]

Most people have a need to tell their story and to feel that it has been understood. Meeting this need can dramatically shift the quality of a relationship, e.g., from a feeling of hostility or mistrust to a feeling of rapport and respect. Meeting this need demonstrates the listener's concern and respect, which tends to defuse anger and mistrust, especially where these emotions stem from feeling unappreciated or exploited. Two-sided messages, in which the listener summarizes the speaker's viewpoint before stating her own, are more persuasive than one-sided messages.[3]

Empathy is the process of demonstrating an accurate, nonjudgmental understanding of the other person's needs, interests, and perspective without necessarily agreeing. Empathy is a "value-neutral mode of observation" or "witnessing," a journey in which you explore and describe another's perceptual world without commitment. Empathizing with someone, therefore, does not mean agreeing with or even necessarily liking the other person. Instead, it simply requires your understanding and acknowledgement of how the world looks to the other person.[4]

Assertiveness is the ability to express and advocate one's own needs, interests, and perspective. It means identifying your own interests, explaining them clearly to the other side, and having the confidence to probe subjects that the other person may prefer to leave untouched.[5]

Empathy and assertiveness are aspects of effective communication. When people communicate well with each other, problem-solving is easier. Therefore, counter-intuitively, if the other side does not want to reciprocate and is reluctant to listen, it is nevertheless in a party's interest to listen effectively to understand and acknowledge the other side's point of view.[6]

Two tools are available that can assist in this endeavor: the ladder of inference and the ladder of accusation.

The **ladder of inference** is a conceptual tool designed to broaden understanding about how and why a person comes to certain conclusions.[7] The simplified ladder consists of three rungs, in ascending order—observations, interpretations, conclusions—and at the base of the ladder is a pool of information.

---

[2] *Id.* at 49.

[3] *Id.* at 49.

[4] *Id.* at 46–47.

[5] *Id.* at 47.

[6] *Id.* at 48.

[7] The ladder of inference was first described by organizational psychologist Chris Argyris and is explained by Peter Senge in THE FIFTH DISCIPLINE: THE ART AND PRACTICE OF THE LEARNING ORGANIZATION (1994).

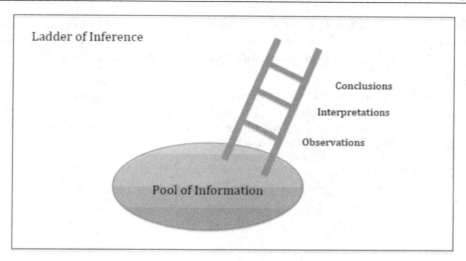

When two parties have come to differing conclusions on a given matter, the ladder of inference can help trace how a party came to her conclusion and why it may differ from another party's conclusion. Parties may be looking at different data, or they may have the same data, but have different interpretations. In either case, their ladders of inference lead them to different conclusions.

For example, some parties interpret the same data differently. Steve is driving down the street and decides that the utility workers he just passed on the side of the road are lazy—a conclusion, which is the third rung up his ladder. The ladder of inference would suggest climbing down the ladder to find out how Steve arrived at his conclusion. Steve may have observed that the utility workers were sitting down under a tree talking—which is the first rung on the ladder. He believes that people who are sitting around talking instead of working are lazy—the second rung up the ladder. So he concludes that the utility workers he observed are lazy. A different observer, Anna, might view the same pool of information as Steve—i.e., utility workers sitting under a tree. But unlike Steve's interpretation, she believes that workers who take occasional breaks are efficient—the second rung on her ladder. She therefore concludes that the utility workers are good, efficient employees.

Alternatively, some parties share beliefs on how to interpret certain data, but they observe different things. Steve may have observed utility workers starting work without consulting a manual, whereas Anna walked by earlier and saw the same workers carefully studying a manual and discussing how to best approach a challenging task. Steve and Anna both believe that consulting plans before working is a smart way to work, but because they observed different data, Steve concludes the utility workers are foolish, while Anna concludes that they are smart.

The ladder of inference doesn't necessarily lead parties to agreement, but it encourages a person to become aware of how she has arrived at her conclusions and to seek to understand how an opposing party may believe differently.

The **ladder of accusation** functions in a manner similar to the ladder of inference. Comprised of four rungs—accusations, demands, requests, and interests—the ladder of accusation is a tool to help a party examine his own or another party's real interests.

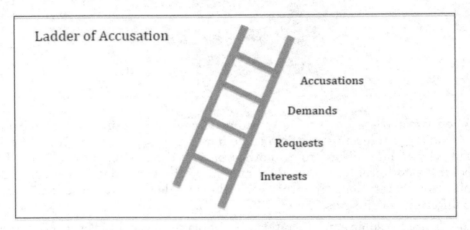

Ladder of Accusation

Accusations

Demands

Requests

Interests

In performative negotiation or mediation, parties often begin on the top rung, with accusations. The ladder of accusation would have a party climb down the ladder (his own or the other party's) to uncover what he (or the other party) really wants. For example, one spouse might accuse another, "You're so selfish!" A rung below, this same notion manifests itself in terms of a demand—e.g., "Spend more time at home!"—which is slightly more helpful than a mere accusation, but still obscuring what the person really wants. Continuing down the ladder, the earlier sentiments become less outward-focused and more inward-looking as they approach the party's true interest, with a request: "I want us to go out one night a week." Finally, the bottom rung represents what the party needs, or his real interest: "I want to spend more time together."

The ladder of accusation allows a party to step down the levels of her (or another's) thinking to discover her real interests. In performative contexts, it can be especially effective in de-escalating a high-conflict, emotional discourse to a more productive conversation about what parties really want.

b. Johari Windows

Joe Luft and Harry Ingham were researching human personality at the University of California in the 1950s when they devised their Johari

Window concepts, named after a combination of their two first names. Their Johari Window concepts are a way of looking at how personality is expressed.

Luft and Ingham observed that there are aspects of our personality about which we open to others, and other aspects that we keep to ourselves. In addition, there are things that others see in us of which we are not aware, and there is a fourth group of things that are unknown now to anyone. These four categories can be illustrated schematically in a four-box grid:[8]

2 Known to others, but not known to me.	3 Not known to me and not known to others.
1 Known to me and known to others.	4 Known to me, but not known to others.

The Johari Window concepts have been extended beyond the expression of human personality to a general-parlance description of what people know and don't know:[9]

1. The public area contains information (e.g., facts, traits, behaviors, etc.) that is openly known (i.e., "what we know").
2. The hidden area contains information that we think others know but we do not know (i.e., "what we don't know").
3. The unknown area contains things that nobody knows (i.e., "what we don't know we don't know").
4. The private area contains information that we know, but choose to keep hidden from others (i.e., "what we know but don't disclose").

The following cartoon illustrates these four categories of our knowledge and its limits in terms of what we and others can and cannot see in four different "rooms:"

---

[8] See generally "Famous Models: Johari Window," http://www.chimaeraconsulting.com/johari.htm

[9] One of the most well-known iterations of this idea was expressed by former U.S. Secretary of Defense Donald Rumsfeld, speaking about Iraq in 2002: "[T]here are known knowns; there are things we know that we know. There are known unknowns; that is to say there are things that we now know we don't know. But there are also unknown unknowns—there are things we do not know we don't know."

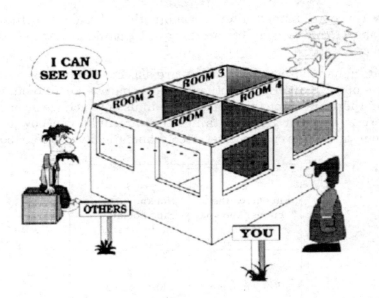

The Johari Window suggests five character traits and related behaviors that (counter-intuitively) are very useful in conflict resolution:

Courage—I should be willing to admit to myself that:

- I may be mistaken about what I think I know.

- I need to learn what you know that I may not know.

- I need to overcome my fear (resistance) of asking you to tell me what you know.

Humility—I should be willing to remind myself that:

- I may be mistaken about what I think I know.

- I should not assume that I know what you know.

- I need to overcome my fear (resistance) of your disclosing information which I do not know.

Trustworthiness—I should be willing to remind myself that:

- I must incentivize you to disclose information which I may not know.

- I must be willing to disclose information to you which you may not know.

- I need to help you overcome your fear (resistance) of your disclosing information which I may not know.

Curiosity—I should be willing to remind myself that:

- You may disclose to me things I do not know that I need to know (even things I don't want to hear).

- You may be mistaken or withholding in what you disclose to me.
- I need to overcome my fear (resistance) of learning what I don't know that I need to know.

Open-mindedness—I should be willing to remind myself that:

- What I learn from you that I need to know may enable me to see you from your perspective.
- What I learn from you that I need to know may enable me to see myself in a new light.
- I need to overcome my fear (resistance) of being affected (changed) by you in disclosing to me what I don't know that I need to know.

It is important to recognize that, in conflict resolution, these five character traits are not soft-hearted or soft-minded, and the behaviors these character traits motivate are not for the timid or the weak. Rather, these character traits and related behaviors are profoundly instrumental in enabling you to promote your self-interest in the midst of conflict.

c. The Contributions of Leonard Hawes to Conflict Analysis and Conflict Resolution

Our colleague, Dr. Leonard Hawes, Professor of Communication at the University of Utah, in a series of as-yet-unpublished manuscripts, has identified a number of unique approaches to conflict analysis and conflict resolution. One approach deals with what we resolve, desire, imagine, will, and resist. These five character traits and related behaviors are implicated in the Johari Windows when:

I must resolve to be clear about what I think I know about our conflict, its causes, my contribution to it, and whether (and, if so, how) I am committed to work to try to resolve it.

I must desire to know what you know that is relevant to my understanding of our conflict that I do not now know but need to know.

I must use my imagination about what may be that relates to the cause of our conflict and its possible resolution.

I must determine my willingness to disclose to you things I think I know which I have kept hidden from you which may relate to the cause of our conflict and its possible resolution.

Finally, **I must deal with my resistance** to use and express my **resolve**, my **desire**, my **imagination**, and my **willingness**.

Hawes suggests four conflict resolution tasks that are the communicative essence of the four strategies of negotiation and mediation discussed in this book:

> First, I must pay attention to complaints (my complaints and your complaints), which often are expressed in our performance of conflict stories, about things that are not working and things I (or you) don't like or don't want. I (and you) then can try to identify the pieces of things that underlie our complaints and accumulate these pieces in what may be described as an "and . . . and . . . and" process that creates (the possibility of) a joint story. This task turns individual performances of monologues into mutual dialogue—real conversation—in the midst of conflict.
>
> I (and you) can explore resolution of our complaints in ways that transform my (and your) understandings of our complaints into new meanings and relationships that are created out of recognition and empowerment. This may be described as an "oh . . . oh . . . oh" transformative process.
>
> I (and you) can look for ways in which the pieces of our complaints (prioritized in categories of relative meaning and relative importance) may come together in patterns (options) of feasibility, acceptability, and durability. This integrative brainstorming may be described as a "so . . . so . . . so" process.
>
> After pieces of our conflict are drawn out and accumulated, they can be sorted in a bargaining-or triage-like manner in terms of what I (and you) prefer or find to be relatively desirable, or not. This may be described as an "or . . . or . . . or" distributive process that ultimately sorts the pieces into categories of agreement, disagreement, and irrelevance.

All the while, I (and you) must be aware of, deal with, and try to overcome the resistance that stands in the way of our accomplishing these four tasks.

Hawes' four tasks are advanced by five lines of useful inquiry, investigation, or questioning:

1. **What do you want?**—This line of inquiry implicates **desire**.
2. **What would it be like if you had what you want?**—This line of inquiry implicates **imagination**.
3. **What have you been willing to do (or say) in order to get what you want?**—This line of inquiry implicates **willingness**.
4. **What have you been unwilling to do (or say) to get what you want?**—This line of inquiry implicates **resistance**.
5. **So, what do you want?**—This line of inquiry implicates **resolve**.

It is important to note that Line of Inquiry #5 is virtually the same as (i.e., the question sounds almost identical to) Line of Inquiry #1. This introduces a *recursive* function into the inquiry (i.e., it is a procedure that can repeat itself indefinitely).

It also should be noted that these questions are lines or strategies of inquiry, and not necessarily specific questions that should be asked in a particular negotiation or mediation. These specific questions, if asked literally, may be appropriate in mediation when raised by a mediator in caucus, but may be off-putting to some people when asked by a party in negotiation and therefore provoke resistance unnecessarily. However, as strategies for asking effective questions whether in negotiation or mediation, these lines of inquiry:

- shift the time frame from past to present (and even to the future);
- motivate (by requesting) first-person, present-tense answers;
- help reveal interests that underlie initial statements of positions; and
- invoke a party's desires and sources of willingness to engage in problem-solving.

d.   Dealing With Emotions: The Five Core Concerns[10]

In negotiation and mediation, "emotions are powerful, always present, and hard to handle."[11] Emotions are a driving force behind much of the action in which parties engage with each other. Emotions can manifest themselves loudly and explicitly, or quietly and subtly. In either case, they can present major obstacles to reaching an agreement. Because many people view law and business as a logical, rational endeavor, they mistakenly attempt to avoid, suppress, or ignore emotion when it comes to creating deals and resolving disputes. Fisher and Shapiro point out that, while it is foolish to ignore emotions, sometimes parties mistakenly think that they should deal directly with all of their emotions in neogtiation.[12] Given the vast range and sheer quantity of emotions that may be at play in the course of any given negotiation or mediation, it is a daunting and sometimes overwhelming task to account for all emotions.[13]

Rather than dealing directly with emotions themselves, Fisher and Shapiro advocate focusing on five "core concerns" that provoke most emotions parties encounter during a negotiation or mediation: *appreciation, affiliation, autonomy, status, and role.*[14]

---

[10] See generally Roger Fisher & Daniel Shapiro, BEYOND REASON (New York: Viking Penguin, 2005).

[11] *Id.* at 3.

[12] *Id.* at 12.

[13] *Id.* at 12–14.

[14] *Id. at 15.*

The Five Core Concerns in Negotiation[15]

Core Concerns	You Feel the Concern Is Ignored When:	You Feel the Concern Is Met When:
Appreciation	Your thoughts, feelings, or actions are devalued by others.	Your thoughts, feelings, and actions are acknowledged.
Affiliation	You are treated as an adversary, with distrust and suspicion.	You are treated as a colleague, with mutual cooperation.
Autonomy	Your freedom to make decisions is impinged upon by others.	Others respect your freedom to make important decisions.
Status	You are treated as being inferior to others.	You are given full recognition where and when deserved.
Role	You or others define your role as unimportant or unfulfilling.	You define your role and activities as fulfilling.

We can show **appreciation** by finding something of value in what the other party thinks, says, or does, and then express it.[16] We can build **affiliation** with the other party by finding common links, such as age, rank, family, religion, background, or interests.[17] We can respect **autonomy** in two ways: 1) expanding our own autonomy, by making recommendations and inventing options; and 2) not impinging on others' autonomy, by always consulting and inviting input before making decisions.[18] We can acknowledge **status** by being respectful and courteous to everyone, looking for each person's area of particular status—in what areas or ways does the person view herself as important—and finding ways to recognize both her high status and our own.[19] Finally, we can choose a fulfilling **role** (or make a conventional role more fulfilling) by identifying its purpose and then shaping the role to include personally meaningful activities.[20]

By becoming aware of and acting to account for these five concerns, negotiators and mediators can better manage emotions as they arise. They can use the five concerns as a preparatory tool to examine

---

[15] *Id.* at 17.

[16] *Id.* at 25.

[17] *Id.* at 54–56.

[18] *Id.* at 72–87.

[19] *Id.* at 94–103.

[20] *Id.* at 115–124.

themselves to see what emotions they anticipate being triggered or affected, and to anticipate the emotions that the other party might experience.[21]

e. Asking Questions

Skilled negotiators and mediators learn to ask questions that drive productive discussion. Asking effective questions can both increase understanding and provide useful information for the party asking the questions, as well as assisting the other party in feeling understood. Because parties in conflict usually approach each other with preconceived judgments and conclusions, it is necessary to ask questions that allow the other party to express his conflict story, and then to explore beneath his positions or accusations to discover his true interests.

Questions should be used purposefully in negotiation and mediation. Negotiators and mediators should become familiar with various types of questions and how they can be used to achieve various goals. For example, open-ended questions (*"How do you feel about what's happened?"*) allow the other party to discuss what is important to her. Clarification questions (*"Do you mean he intentionally did this?"*) can be used to ensure understanding, challenge assumptions, or encourage the party to climb down her ladder of inference or accusation (see the discussion in the previous section).

The following are other examples of types of questions that can be employed for particular purposes:

- Ask questions that test the underlying emotion: *"Do you feel sad about this?"*
- Ask questions about the speaker's underlying interests: *"What do you want?"*
- Ask expansive questions: *"Would you explain more about what you want?"* or *"Would you help me understand why that's important to you?"*
- Ask operational questions: *"What is a good way to accomplish this?"* or *"How can we work together to come up with some solutions that will meet both of our interests?"*
- Ask commitment questions: *"Would you be willing to . . .?"*

Asking effective questions becomes an especially powerful tool when paired with effective listening.

f. Effective Listening

Of all the skills available to negotiators and mediators, effective listening may be the most important. Without active listening, productive

---

[21] *Id.* at 19–20.

communication is extremely difficult, if not impossible. Negotiators who are able to listen effectively increase the likelihood of overcoming impasses, understanding their own and the other side's interests, and generating more options that better satisfy their own and the other party's interests. Mediators who listen effectively are more likely to understand the interests of the parties and better position themselves to help move the parties toward a settlement that is satisfactory to both sides.

Listening is an attitude and a choice implemented by four kinds of behaviors:

1. **Attending Behaviors:**
   - Maintain appropriate posture and proximity to the other person.
   - Make empathetic eye contact and empathic facial expressions.
   - Use encouraging nonverbal expressions (e.g., head nodding).

2. **Inviting Behaviors:**
   - Listen without interrupting, judging, or preparing to talk.
   - Use encouraging verbal expressions (e.g., "uh-huh," "okay," "I see").
   - Encourage the other person to continue talking (e.g., "tell me more about . . . ").

3. **Confirming Behaviors:**
   - Ask follow-up questions with sincere curiosity to get additional information.
   - Show that you understand the other person's feelings (i.e., emotional affect).
   - Acknowledge that you find something of merit in what you have heard.

4. **Summarizing Behaviors:**
   - Briefly summarize what you have heard, using the other person's key words and feelings.
   - Ask whether your summary is correct and complete.
   - If not, revise your summary and re-ask whether your summary is correct and complete.

While listening, on its own, does not create deals and resolve disputes, it serves as the facilitating factor that enables productive communication to take place. Parties that are unable to communicate productively are unlikely to find outcomes that are durable or satisfactory, so effective listening is an essential component to negotiation and mediation.

g. Reframing[22]

People in conflict often frame their experience as a conflict story that blames and stereotypes the other person: *"You forced me to quit because of a hostile workplace. I had to quit because you are a racist."* The other person often responds with a denial and a counter conflict story: *"That's not true. You are lazy and incompetent and you couldn't do the work. That's why you quit."* The two continue back and forth in an unproductive spiral of inflammatory exchanges. Reframing is one way to break out of this downward spiral and direct the discussion toward a more productive path by stripping out the speaker's negative emotion and accusatory language and restating the speaker's underlying interests. For example, a mediator could reframe the conflict story and the counter conflict story into a third story: *"You both seem upset that the employment situation did not work out."*

Reframing can be used as a tool in negotiation and mediation that leads to more productive communication between parties because it facilitates the following:

- Reframing focuses on the parties' problem, not on the character of the persons involved.
- Reframing engages the speaker's willingness to look at the problem from a new perspective.
- Reframing enables the other person to hear and acknowledge the speaker's concerns.
- Reframing opens up the opportunity for dialogue about unexpressed needs or fears.
- Reframing increases the likelihood of mutual problem-solving.

The following are ways to approach reframing:

- Listen carefully to the statement.
- Try to identify the speaker's underlying interests or concerns.
- Recognize the speaker's underlying emotion (e.g., anger or sadness).
- Try to find the speaker's positive intent hiding behind the underlying emotion.
- Strip out the accusatory language.
- Change negative words into neutral or positive words.
- Express a complaint as a request (e.g., for a change in the relationship).
- Restate the statement as the speaker's concern about underlying, unexpressed needs or fears.

---

[22] See, e.g., William Ury, *Don't Reject: Reframe*, GETTING PAST NO: NEGOTIATING WITH DIFFICULT PEOPLE 76–104 (New York: Bantam Books, 1991),

Because a party may, at any point, say something inflammatory (whether deliberately or inadvertently) that could derail the discussion, reframing can be useful throughout the negotiation or mediation process.

EXERCISE

A "Conflict Stories" Conversation in Performative Negotiation

This exercise illustrates what can happen in a conversation involving conflict stories.

You and a partner should assume fictional names: one of you is "Smith" and the other is "Jones." Smith should read the "Confidential Information for Smith" which is on the following page. Jones should read the "Confidential Information for Jones" which is on the second page following this one.

Begin the conversation and stop after about five minutes. After you stop the conversation, discuss with your partner what you experienced.

"The Biting Dog" Conversation in Performative Negotiation

Confidential Information for Smith

Background facts for Smith:

Your neighbor Jones has a large pit bull dog in the front yard which is fenced but has an unlocked gate. You have complained many times to your neighbor about keeping such a dangerous dog in an unlocked yard.

You have a three-year-old child. You were home alone with your child and you took a nap on the couch. While you were asleep, your child opened the back door of your house, went next door, opened the unlocked gate, went inside the fence, and was bit by the pit bull. You heard your child's screams, ran next door, and took your child to the hospital, where your child received stitches.

Instructions for Smith:

You are furious: Jones is to blame for keeping such a dangerous dog that hurt your child. Stay in role; talk at Jones while Jones is trying to talk to you; keep repeating your story; do not attempt to resolve this problem.

"The Beaten Dog" Conversation in Performative Negotiation

Confidential Information for Jones

Background facts for Jones:

You have an American Staffordshire terrier dog in your front yard, which is fenced with a closed gate. Your neighbor Smith has a three-year-old child who has come unattended into your yard several times to play. You have complained to Smith that the child should not be allowed to come into your yard.

Smith was home alone with the child. Instead of supervising the child, Smith took a nap. While Smith slept, Smith's child got out of the house, opened your gate, went inside your fence, teased and hit your dog with a big stick, and was bitten by your sweet dog in self-defense. Smith woke up from the nap, ran into your yard, and pulled the child away.

Instructions for Jones:

You are furious: Smith is negligent for sleeping while the child came unattended into your fenced yard through your closed gate and got hurt while beating your dog through no fault of yours. Stay in role; talk at Smith while Smith is trying to talk to you; keep repeating your story; do not attempt to resolve this problem.

B. TRANSFORMATIVE PRINCIPLES

The transformative strategy is a focus on the relationship between the parties. The transformative approach looks for ways to improve communication between parties in a way that improves their relationship. As the relationship improves, the parties become empowered and willing to solve their dispute. The primary goal in this strategy is not necessarily to come to agreement of the parties' specific (presenting) conflict, but to transform the relationship between the parties in a way that makes ongoing agreements about conflict more likely.

1. IN NEGOTIATION

Parties in conflict who employ the transformative strategy likely have begun negotiating in an unproductive way. There may be a history of emotional, ineffective communication that has soured the parties' relationship, making it difficult for the sides to discuss the matter without anger. In this high-conflict context, the relationship between the parties prevents them from coming anywhere near an agreement that would be satisfactory to both sides. A transformative negotiator would recognize the importance of changing the relationship before focusing on coming to an agreement. He would concentrate on active listening and employ other transformative mediation tools (discussed in the section below) to change the conversation in a way that allows the parties to experience mutual empowerment. When parties have a strong sense of self and their common humanity, they open up space for them to negotiate toward an agreement on issues that had previously become severely entrenched.

Transformative negotiation has a unique process. Unlike integrative and distributive negotiation, which tend to follow (even if loosely) a series of steps, transformative negotiation proceeds in a more unstructured, free-flowing manner. Because the parties are focusing on their relationship, the range of relevant issues to discuss tends to be much greater than the issues typically encountered in other types of negotiation, which are more defined and limited to the context of the particular deal or dispute.

The transformative approach is most relevant for negotiating parties whose history of conflict has resulted in a deteriorating relationship. While it is certainly possible for one party to break free from a downward spiral of ineffective communication and change to a transformative strategy, many will find it extremely difficult to do so on their own. Accordingly, transformative situations are especially conducive to mediator involvement, which is explored in greater depth below.

2.   IN MEDIATION[23]

The authors Bush and Folger emphasize that parties involved in what appears at first to be a single "conflict" may be seeking different kinds of help from different kinds of interveners and may be expecting that their conflict will be resolved in different ways. Therefore, a mediator, who is asked to intervene to help parties in the middle of a conflict, must reflect on two basic, interrelated questions:

1. What kind of help does each party need and want from the mediator?
2. What is each party's theory of the nature of the conflict and how it should be resolved?

Bush and Folger believe there are three traditional theories of the nature of conflict and how conflict should be resolved:

- **Power–Based Conflicts**. A party may be seeking help in consolidating *power* in order to control another party (or to resist that party's domination) and therefore is expecting a power-based theory of conflict intervention.
- **Rights–Based Conflicts**. A party may be seeking help in vindicating *rights* and therefore be expecting a rights-based theory of conflict intervention.
- **Needs–Based Conflicts**. A party may seek help in satisfying *needs* and therefore be expecting an interest-based theory of conflict intervention.

Because conflicts often implicate power, rights, and needs, three different theories of conflict intervention are implicated. However, according to Bush and Folger, a mediator (based on her past experience and training) tends to see just one kind of conflict and therefore tends to use just one kind of conflict intervention (which may differ from what the parties expect or need). Some mediators may assume that parties are engaged in power-based conflicts and therefore assume they seek protection from domination. Other mediators may assume that parties are engaged in rights-based conflicts and therefore assume they seek to vindicate rights. Other mediators may assume that parties are engaged in needs-based conflicts and therefore assume they seek to satisfy important needs and interests. Similarly, parties tend to choose a mediator who they believe sees their particular kind of conflict and who therefore will use the kind of conflict intervention they expect and want.

According to the transformative view of conflict, although parties in conflict may be frustrated in their pursuit of power, rights, or needs, they

---

[23]   See generally Robert A. Baruch Bush & Joseph P. Folger, The Promise of Mediation: The Transformative Approach to Conflict (rev. ed.) at 41–84 (San Francisco: Jossey–Bass Publishers, 2005).

more importantly feel their strength is undermined in their deteriorating interactions and they feel alienated from one another. Therefore, they feel weak and self-absorbed and they need a transformative mediator's help in overcoming their interactional crisis. Transformative mediation minimizes the parties' feelings of powerlessness and alienation by maximizing their decision making and communication.

Research in cognitive and social psychology and neurophysiology confirms that parties in conflict experience their sense of relative weakness as lost control, confusion, doubt, uncertainty, and indecisiveness. They experience their self-absorption as being more protective of themselves and more suspicious and closed to the perspective of others. These feelings create a downward negative conflict spiral: the weaker that parties feel, the more self-absorbed they become. This creates a vicious cycle that escalates their conflict.

Conflict throws into question the sense of identity that underscores a person's life, i.e., that of a strong self, meaningfully connected to others. The sense of weakness and alienation caused by interactional conflict threatens this core identity. To remain in such a condition is inhuman, which is a powerful *motivation* to change.

Bush and Folger believe that parties therefore need and want the intervention of a mediator who will help reverse their downward negative conflict spiral and help them restore constructive interactions. Parties sometimes express this as their desire for "closure," i.e., they want to get past the embittered experience of conflict and move on with their lives, whether together or apart. They want to move out of their negative interactions by reversing their downward conflict spiral, even if this means they do not reach agreement on the substantive issues (i.e., power, rights, or interests) involved in their conflict.

Bush and Folger believe that the critical resource in transformative mediation is the parties' basic humanity, especially their strength (their agency and individual autonomy) and their compassion (their social connection and understanding). When parties activate these basic human capacities, they reverse their downward conflict spiral and create positive interactions, even without the help of a mediator. They move out of their sense of weakness and become more confident, articulate, and decisive, which Bush and Folger call the process of "empowerment." They also move out of their self-absorption and become more attentive, open, and understanding, which Bush and Folger call the process of "recognition."

The processes of empowerment and recognition lead to an upward positive cycle: the stronger I feel, the more open I am to you; this helps you feel stronger and more open to me; and so on. These processes transform the way the parties experience themselves and the ways they interact with each other. The mediator helps these processes along by supporting each party's small but critical shifts from weakness to strength and from self-absorption to understanding.

Bush and Folger contrast the mediator's role in traditional mediation with that in transformative mediation. In traditional mediation, the mediator is an impartial third party who establishes ground rules, identifies issues, develops an agenda, helps generate options, and helps the parties achieve a mutually acceptable resolution of some or all of the issues in dispute. By contrast, in transformative mediation, the mediator helps the parties move from negative and destructive interactions to positive and constructive ones. The transformative mediator helps the parties make shifts in empowerment and recognition by supporting their exercise of their capacities for strength and connection. Empowerment shifts tend to occur first as the capacity for strength asserts itself. Shifts in recognition occur next as the capacity for connection asserts itself. These shifts of empowerment and recognition are not smooth and even, because parties in conflict tend to fall back into weakness and self-absorption.

Bush and Folger believe the mediator's role in transformative mediation is to ensure that parties are responsible for their outcomes and to support their competence and motives. Transformative mediators avoid taking sides, expressing judgments, being directive, giving advice, or acting as advocates. Supporting the parties' empowerment and recognition shifts is more important than their achieving a settlement. Transformative mediation reestablishes the parties' strength and self-confidence and their sense of decency and common humanity. By making positive changes in their interactions, parties themselves often resolve the substantive issues involved in their conflict, without the mediator having to address those. Through transformative mediation, parties ultimately become more capable in resolving other conflicts, which also creates greater social capacity in transforming conflicts.

a.   Facilitating a Transformative Mediation[24]

The core purpose of transformative mediation is for the mediator to support and help parties as they engage in their own difficult conversations about whatever is important to them, thereby transforming their relationship. In transformative mediation, the parties are responsible for both conducting the process and determining the outcome. In contrast to other kinds of mediation, transformative mediation is an unstructured, unfolding conversation between the parties which is facilitated by the mediator, rather than a structured sequence of ordered stages through which the mediator moves the parties toward conflict resolution and settlement.

---

[24]   See generally Bush & Folger, *supra* note 23, at 109–19.

In transformative mediation, the mediator invites the parties to:

- design and redesign the mediation process to be continually responsive to the goals they want to accomplish;
- discuss or at least suggest what they want to be the guidelines or ground rules for their conversation;
- discuss their expectations about confidentiality and any other commitments they might make to each other at the beginning of the mediation;
- engage in different kinds of difficult conversation, in no specified order, to explore their interactional situation, discuss possible new ways of interacting, deliberate about what they might do differently in the future, and make decisions about going forward; and
- as they share new information and create new contexts between themselves, cycle back to and re-explore earlier parts of their conversation.

The core purpose of transformative mediation (i.e., to support and help parties as they engage in their own difficult conversations about whatever is important to them) drives mediator practice. The mediator in transformative mediation:

- believes and trusts that the parties are capable of making their own good decisions and overcoming whatever conflict issues exist between them;
- focuses on closely following the parties' conversation nonjudgmentally as it unfolds moment by moment, using "deep" listening (i.e., listening with an open, curious, interested mind that is free of distractions, interpretations, judgments, assumptions, and conclusions) in addition to using active listening behaviors;
- looks for opportunities to help the parties' become more confident, articulate, and decisive (i.e., opportunities for empowerment shifts);
- looks for opportunities to help the parties' become more attentive, open, and understanding (i.e., opportunities for recognition shifts);
- looks for opportunities for empowerment and recognition that are contained in the parties' expressions of ambiguity, confusion, and uncertainty, and especially in their negative expressions about weakness and accusation; and
- helps the parties become clearer about their own views, the other's perspectives, and their options, available resources, and choices.

3.   TRANSFORMATIVE SKILLS

The following are tools or skills that can be developed and employed in any negotiation or mediation, but tend to be especially relevant to the transformative approach, given its focus on relationships.

The Toolbox:

- Effectively Navigating Difficult Conversations
- Apology and Forgiveness
- Body Language and Nonverbal Communication

a.   Effectively Navigating Difficult Conversations

One of the biggest challenges in many negotiations and mediations is for parties to communicate about difficult issues in a way that is productive. Often parties get mired down in the details of who said or did what and they become locked in a performative back-and-forth verbal battle that deepens and entrenches negative thoughts and feelings toward the other party. How to talk to each other in a way that is likely to lead to satisfactory outcomes for both parties is elusive.

In *Difficult Conversations*,[25] authors Stone, Patton, and Heen construct a framework for analyzing, preparing for, and conducting discussions to confront and resolve the vast array of challenging issues we may encounter as we interact with others. They posit that any difficult conversation involves three separate conversations:

1. The What–Happened Conversation
2. The Feelings Conversation
3. The Identity Conversation

i.   *The What–Happened Conversation*[26]

Difficult conversations are almost never about getting the facts right—though we often mistakenly assume that is what matters most. What generally lie at the heart of difficult conversations are conflicting perceptions, interpretations, and values. We get caught up in a fog of disputed facts and insist on imposing our version of what happened on the other party, without realizing that arguing without first understanding the other side is unpersuasive. People almost never change without first being understood.

Mistaken assumptions about the other party's intentions also color our view of the dispute. We assume we know the intentions of others when we don't. Because intentions are invisible, we often "invent" other people's

---

[25] Douglas Stone, Bruce Patton & Sheila Heen, DIFFICULT CONVERSATIONS: HOW TO DISCUSS WHAT MATTERS MOST (New York: Penguin Books, 2000).

[26] *Id.* at 25–82.

intentions. I try to infer your intentions from your behavior, and I assume the best about me and the worst about you. When I play the Blame Game, I say: "It's your fault; I am blameless." In most difficult conversations, parties focus on the past and on who's to blame. You feel I'm attacking you, so you defend yourself. You then attack me and I defend myself. This continues back and forth in a death spiral, and any hope for productive discussion evaporates in the heat of anger, defensiveness, and other negative emotions.

Stone, Patton, and Heen recommend the following three steps to deal effectively with the What Happened conversation:[27]

1. *Stop arguing about who's right and, instead, explore each other's stories.* Each party has a story that is a reflection of the way she views the world and what happened. Change your position from one of certainty in your own story to one of curiosity about the other party's story. Become genuinely curious about why the other party has come to such a radically different conclusion than your own and ask questions to elicit information that would enable you to gain a better understanding of her story.

2. *Don't assume they meant it—disentangle intent from impact.* There are two things we know: our intent, and the impact of another party's actions on us. There are two things we don't know: the other party's intent, and the impact of our actions on them. We need to recognize this and refrain from assuming that, because the impact of their actions on us was bad, they intended it to be bad, and that because our intentions were good, the impact of our actions on the other party must have been good. Share with the other party the impact of their actions and inquire about their intentions. Also, listen to and acknowledge the other party's feelings, and reflect on your intentions. While you may believe your intentions are pure, be open to the fact that intentions can be complex and there may be more at play than you initially had realized or admitted.

3. *Abandon blame—map the contribution system.* Blame looks backward; contribution looks forward. If we focus on blame we prevent ourselves from coming to a better understanding of the other party's perspective and of the dispute as a whole. Mapping contribution means acknowledging that both parties share responsibility for what happened, and should therefore work together to find out what went wrong and how to prevent something similar from happening again. Our contribution might be very minimal, but by acknowledging and taking responsibility for it, we can encourage the other party to reciprocate. When we

---

[27] *Id.*

focus on contribution we better enable ourselves and the other party to engage in joint problem-solving.

ii.   The Feelings Conversation[28]

Feelings often are at the heart of difficult conversations. Understanding feelings, talking about feelings, and managing feelings are among the greatest challenges of being human. Sometime parties in a dispute will try to ignore feelings (their own or the other party's) or to suppress them, but unexpressed feelings have a way of emerging into and controlling the conversation. Our unexpressed feelings make it difficult to listen to the other party, and they make it difficult for us to engage in problem-solving. Stone, Patton, and Heen emphasize that we need to deal with our feelings and recommend the following:

1. First, find out what your feelings are. Sometimes we often don't know how we feel, because feelings can be hidden, masked, and bundled in a complex of emotions. Feelings often take the shape of judgments or attributions of blame, so we can use the urge to blame as a signal to explore what feelings are underlying those urges.[29]

2. Next, negotiate with your feelings. Our feelings follow our thoughts, so we can change our feelings by changing our thoughts. This involves reconsidering our version of what happened and thinking about what the other party's story might look like and why it makes sense to them. We should also question to what extent our feelings are based on untested assumptions about the other party's intentions, and consider the ways in which we might be contributing to the problem. When we think through these issues, though we may not come up with definitive answers, it may soften and change our feelings, even if only moderately.[30]

3. Finally, describe your feelings carefully. In other words, don't just vent, but express how you are feeling without judging or attributing blame. Stone, Patton, and Heen recommend using the phrase "I feel . . ." as a way to share feelings effectively, because it "keeps the focus on feelings and makes clear that you are speaking only from your perspective."[31]

Acknowledging the other party's feelings is a critical part of effectively navigating a difficult conversation. We can acknowledge feelings by ex-

---

[28] *Id.* at 83–108.
[29] *Id.* at 91–99.
[30] *Id.* at 99–101.
[31] *Id.* at 105.

pressing our understanding of what the other party has shared and letting them know that their feelings matter.[32]

iii. The Identity Conversation[33]

Another fundamental aspect of a difficult conversation is the way it threatens our idea of who we are. We all have constructed a story about ourselves that we share with the world and tell ourselves. This story is our identity. Difficult conversations can threaten to disrupt, alter, or fundamentally change this story, which leads to fear, anxiety, and defensiveness. While people have a large range of identities (identifications), Stone, Patton, and Heen identify three core identities that tend to be at the heart of many disputes: competence, integrity, and self-worth.[34] These three core identities are implicated when, in conflict, we are confronted with the following questions:

1. Am I competent?
2. Am I a good person?
3. Am I worthy of love?

We can more successfully manage our identity issues when we become aware that our identity is an issue in conflict, and we realize that our identities are complex. We run into trouble when we view our identities as all-or-nothing—I'm either competent or I'm a failure, I'm good or I'm bad, etc. One way to overcome this perspective is by adopting what the authors call the "And Stance." Because we are all an amalgam of both positive and negative qualities, we can recognize this by saying to ourselves, for example, "I am a good writer, AND I was sloppy in this instance and made some embarrassing grammatical mistakes."[35] We should also remember that the other party is also dealing with identity issues, too, and recognize that her reactions may be her attempts to manage our threats to her identity.[36]

iv. Creating a Learning Conversation

By taking the three conversations into account, we can have what Stone, Patton, and Heen call a "learning conversation." The learning conversation involves five steps:

1. *Walk through the Three Conversations* (what happened, feelings, and identity).[37] Prepare for a difficult conversation by reviewing the three conversations and thinking through the issues associat-

---

[32] *Id.* at 106.

[33] *Id.* at 109–128.

[34] *Id.* at 116.

[35] *Id.* at 116–128,

[36] *Id.* at 126.

[37] *Id.* at 217–220.

ed with each. Consider each party's contribution and explore alternative interpretations of both parties' intentions and impact.

2. *Check your purpose.*[38] We need to make sure that we know what we are hoping to get out of the conversation. We can't change other people and, though we can hope someone will change, we are likely to escalate the problem or remain frustrated and disappointed if our primary goal is to change the other party. We are more likely to have a productive conversation and be satisfied with its outcome if our goal is mutual understanding. Stone, Patton, and Heen also point out that not all issues are best resolved through talking. Sometimes, as we sort through the three conversations, we realize that the problem is more of an internal issue that is best handled on our own.

3. *Start from the Third Story.*[39] Each party has her own perspective on what happened, and typically we start conversations with our own story, which often involves judgments about the other party and justifications for why we're right and they're wrong. The Third Story is a neutral, more objective version of the two parties' stories, framed in a way that both could agree captures the essence of the dispute. When we start a conversation with our own story, it tends to make the other side defensive, reactive, and even angry. Starting from the Third Story starts the conversation in the right direction and sets the right tone by creating space for each party to share their feelings and perspectives in a way that is less judgmental, blaming, and threatening. Stone, Patton, and Heen suggest opening with a phrase like, "My sense is that you and I see this situation differently. I'd like to share how I'm seeing it, and learn more about how you're seeing it."[40]

4. *Explore their story and yours.*[41] The Three Conversations can provide a framework for what the parties should talk about, including exploring where the stories come from, sharing the impact of the other party's words or actions on each other, describing feelings, and openly discussing identity issues.[42] Stone, Patton, and Heen advocate a range of skills that are conducive to fostering productive dialogue, including active listening, becoming genuinely curious about the other party's story, asking open-ended questions, asking for concrete information (i.e., specific details or examples), paraphrasing to demonstrate your understanding of the other's

---

[38] *Id.* at 131–146; 220.

[39] *Id.* at 221–222.

[40] *Id.* at 152.

[41] *Id.* at 222–230.

[42] *Id.* at 161.

perspective, and reframing to keep the conversation on a productive path.[43]

In addition to helping the other person communicate effectively, we need to express ourselves clearly. Our task is not to persuade, impress, trick, outwit, convert, or win the other party over; rather, we need to express what we see and how we feel. We should start by sharing what matters most—what is important to us. We shouldn't present our conclusions as *the truth*, but instead share our conclusions as *our conclusions*. We should disclose our assumptions and the observations on which our conclusions are based. Sometimes this means we must share our life experiences and values that influence what we think and how we feel. We can help the other party understand us by asking them to paraphrase what they've heard.[44]

5. *Engage in joint problem-solving.*[45] Problem-solving involves exchanging information, testing perceptions, creating options that meet our primary concerns, and finding fair ways to resolve differences. I may have to make some compromises and concessions to meet your needs. Because there are two people involved, it takes both to reach agreement. I need to tell you what would persuade me and ask you what would persuade you. I can ask, "What if . . . ?" I can ask your advice. I can ask what standards apply. If we can't find a creative way to solve the problem, we need to find and apply fair principles. If we still can't agree, we should discuss what interests and concerns are not met by the solutions we have proposed, which may lead to new options. If we still can't agree, we should discuss our alternatives, and we need to be willing to accept the consequences of our failure to reach agreement. We also may need to allow more time to work together.[46]

b. Apology and Forgiveness

People in conflict often feel "stuck" and unable to move on. Some people in conflict feel guilt, remorse, and a desire to make restitution or do equity, but they are afraid to relinquish their pride, express their shame, and admit that they were wrong. Repentance is difficult to do, because it "is the remorseful acceptance of responsibility for one's wrongful and harmful actions, the repudiation of the aspects of one's character that generated the actions, the resolve to do one's best to extirpate those

---

[43] *Id.* at 163–184.

[44] *Id.* at 185–200.

[45] *Id.* at 230–232.

[46] *Id.* at 201–216.

aspects of one's character, and the resolve to atone or make amends for the harm that one has done."[47]

Other people in conflict feel unresolved anger, fear, and vengefulness on the one hand, or helplessness, victimization, and alienation on the other. They tend to hold on to their anger or fear with an attitude of righteous indignation, which justifies their refusal to change. To them, "forgiveness means 'giving up all hope of having a better past.' "[48]

People in conflict want to be healed, to regain control of their life stories, and to be able to move on with their lives. To do this, they must be willing to make a sacrifice, e.g., either to apologize and make restitution on the one hand, or forgive and let go of righteous indignation and vengefulness on the other.

One powerful sacrifice is to make a sincere expression of apology, empathy, or regret. To apologize is to sacrifice one's pride, feel shame, and admit that one is not blameless. Three key elements of making an effective apology include:

1. Recognize the emotional impact of your negative action on others.
2. Express sincere regret for your negative action.
3. Commit not to repeat your negative action.[49]

In addition to apology, another powerful healing tool is forgiveness. Forgiveness means letting go of anger or resentment, sometimes accompanied by greater empathy for the point of view of the person who has harmed us. It is a choice not to let past grievances compromise our future by clogging our thoughts and emotions. It does not mean denying harm, or necessarily letting the person or people you forgive back into your life or even speaking directly with them. As Kenneth Cloke describes, forgiveness is something we can do to help ourselves:

> Forgiveness is not something we do for someone else, but to free ourselves from unhealthy pain, anger, and shame. Anger gives the appearance of being powerful, but leaves us feeling frustrated and powerless. Forgiveness appears weak, but leaves us feeling stronger and less vulnerable to others. Forgiveness is a gift to our own peace of mind, our self-esteem, our relationships with others, and our future. It frees us from entanglement in the past. It helps us reestablish control over our lives by letting go of unpleasant events

---

[47] Jeffrie G. Murphy, GETTING EVEN: FORGIVENESS AND ITS LIMITS 41 (New York: Oxford University Press, 2003).

[48] Kenneth Cloke, MEDIATING DANGEROUSLY: THE FRONTIERS OF CONFLICT RESOLUTION 90 (San Francisco: Jossey–Bass Publishers, 2001).

[49] Roger Fisher & Daniel Shapiro, BEYOND REASON: USING EMOTIONS AS YOU NEGOTIATE 163 (New York: Viking, 2005).

and people, and by reconnecting us with healthier, more positive people and directions.[50]

The following five benefits of forgiveness go not to the person who is forgiven, but to the person who forgives:[51]

1. Reduced stress

When we mentally replay a hurtful memory or nurse a grudge against a person who mistreated or offended us, the body reacts with a stress response. You can't change the past, but changing how you think about the hurtful past can reduce its impact on you and the resulting likelihood of stress-related illness.

2. A change of heart

Willingness to forgive may lower your heart disease risk. In laboratory studies at the University of Tennessee, forgiving a parent or friend for a betrayal was associated with lower blood pressure, lower heart rate, and a reduced workload for the heart muscle.

3. Stronger relationships

Partners in long-term relationships often hurt one another. Developing a capacity for forgiveness can help keep small disappointments from developing into big ones. Regularly practicing forgiveness toward those with whom you live can keep small incidents from hardening into lingering resentment.

4. Help with pain and chronic illness

Faced with pain or chronic illness, we sometimes respond with anger, frustration, self-blame, or guilt for the effect of the illness on loved ones, and grief at the loss of a healthy life. The ability to forgive yourself, your pain, or your illness may help promote healing.

5. Greater happiness

When you forgive someone, you make yourself—rather than the person who hurt you—responsible for your future happiness, because you are no longer fixed on righting the wrong or getting even.

c. Body Language and Nonverbal Communication

Skilled negotiators and mediators pay attention to body language and nonverbal cues. "Often, more is told in the way a person says something than in what they actually say."[52] People communicate significant

---

[50] Kenneth Cloke, MEDIATING DANGEROUSLY: THE FRONTIERS OF CONFLICT RESOLUTION 94 (San Francisco: Jossey–Bass Publishers, 2001).

[51] See generally *Five for 2005: Five Reasons to Forgive*, 12 HARVARD WOMEN'S HEALTH WATCH 5 (Harvard Medical School, January 2005).

[52] John W. Kennish, *How to Read Body Language: Non–Verbal Cues Can Turn into Clues That Help Lead You to the Truth*, at 28, 29, PA. LAW. (Nov/Dec 1995).

amounts of information nonverbally—mostly unintentionally. By watching how parties cross their arms or legs, what they do with their hands, where they look, etc., sometimes you can get a sense of what they are thinking or how they are feeling even if they haven't verbally expressed those thoughts or feelings.

Cynthia Lardner provides a list of various types of body language and their potential associated meanings:[53]

NONVERBAL BEHAVIOR	INTERPRETATION
Standing with hands on hips	Readiness, aggression
Sitting with legs crossed, foot kicking slightly	Boredom
Sitting, legs apart	Open, relaxed
Arms crossed on chest	Defensiveness
Hand to cheek	Evaluation, thinking
Touching, slightly rubbing nose	Rejection, doubt, lying
Rubbing the eye	Doubt, disbelief
Hands clasped behind back	Anger, frustration, apprehension
Locked ankles	Apprehension
Head resting in hand, eyes downcast	Boredom
Rubbing hands	Anticipation
Sitting with hands clasped behind head	Confidence, superiority
Tapping or drumming fingers	Impatience
Patting/fondling hair	Lack of self-confidence; insecurity
Tilted head	Interest
Stroking chin	Trying to make a decision
Looking down, face turned away	Disbelief
Pulling or lugging at ear	Indecision

---

[53] See generally Cynthia Marie–Martinovich Lardner, *What You Didn't Say Speaks Volumes*, MICH. B.J. at 36, 38 (October 2002).

Jeffrey Krivis and Mariam Zadeh suggest that reading nonverbal cues can be an important skill in determining whether another party is attempting to deceive you.[54] They provide a list of cues from sociology, psychology, and communications research which are intended to help you recognize when another party is being deceitful. Some of these cues include the following:

- Increased pupil dilation—Deceivers' pupils tend to widen as they would in dim lighting.

- Blinking—Deceivers tend to blink more frequently when compared to individuals telling the truth.

- Eye shifting—Deceivers will tend to look away, up, down, or to the side, rather than at the person they are addressing.

- Self-adaptors—Deceivers tend to use their hands to fondle or manipulate objects or parts of their body.

- Leg gesturing and swiveling in chairs—Deceivers tend to have more leg twitches, tapping feet, and will either swivel or rock when sitting.

- Less hand and head gesturing—Deceivers "speak" less with their hands and tend to keep their head still.[55]

Reading body language is an imperfect art. Although certain gestures or positions may often signal particular messages, sometimes crossed arms are just crossed arms (e.g., crossed arms may be indicating the room is cold rather than the party is defensive). Therefore, you should be cautious in relying too heavily on specific interpretations. Nonetheless, mediators and negotiators should pay attention to body language. Deciphering nonverbal cues can aid in "reading" another party and provide valuable insights into the other party's thoughts and feelings.

EXERCISE

Identify a conflict you have now or once had with someone who is important to you. (The greater the conflict and the more important the person is to you, the better this example is to analyze.) Ask that person if, for the purpose of this exercise, he or she would be willing to be audiotaped talking with you about the conflict. Tell the person you are going to prepare a transcript of a portion of the conversation to use to analyze **how you communicate** in the audiotaped conversation. You are not going to analyze how the other person communicates.

1. Arrange a time a place to have the conversation that should be uninterrupted by telephone calls or other persons. Audiotape the conversation.

---

[54] Jeffrey Krivis & Mariam Zadeh, *Back to Deception: "Winning" Mediation Cases by Understanding Body Language*, 24 ALTERNATIVES TO HIGH COST LITIG. 113 (2006).

[55] *Id.* at 122–123.

2. Listen to the audiotape. Select about five minutes of the audiotaped conversation that is important to you.

3. Prepare a deposition-like transcript of the selected five-minute portion of the audiotape, i.e., on each page of the transcript, number each line on the page, and identify when you are talking and when the other person is talking:

<u>Line</u>

1   You: _____

2   _____

3   _____

4   Other: _____

5   _____

6   _____

7   You: _____

8   _____

9   _____

4. By referring to specific portions of the transcript and using relevant concepts from this book, analyze what you are doing in the conversation.

EXERCISE

A "Conflict Stories" Conversation in Transformative Negotiation

This exercise illustrates what can happen in a conflict conversation in which important relationships are valued.

You and a partner should assume fictional names: one of you is "Smith" and the other is "Jones." Smith should read the "Confidential Information for Smith" on the following page. Jones should read the "Confidential Information for Jones" which is on the second page following this one.

Conduct your conversation for about five minutes. After you stop the conversation, discuss with your partner what you experienced.

"The Dangerous Dog" Conversation in Transformative Negotiation

Confidential Information for Smith

Background facts for Smith:

Your neighbor Jones has a large pit bull dog in the front yard which is fenced but has an unlocked gate. You have complained many times to your neighbor about keeping a dangerous dog in an unlocked yard.

You have a three-year-old child. You were home alone with your child and you took a nap on the couch. While you were asleep, your child opened the back door of your house, went next door, opened the unlocked gate, went inside the fence, and was bitten by the dog. You heard your child's screams, ran next door, and took your child to the hospital, where your child received multiple stitches.

Instructions for Smith:

You are angry but concerned: Jones is to blame for keeping such a dangerous dog that hurt your child. However, Jones has been a good neighbor and you want to preserve the relationship. Talk to Jones about what happened and how you want to preserve your relationship with Jones.

"The Negligent Parent" Conversation in Transformative Negotiation

Confidential Information for Jones

Background facts for Jones:

You have a American Staffordshire terrier dog in your front yard which is fenced with a closed gate. Your neighbor Smith has a three year-old child who has come unattended into your yard several times to play. You have complained to Smith that the child should not be allowed to come into your yard.

Smith was home alone with the child. Instead of supervising the child, Smith took a nap. While Smith slept, Smith's child got out of the house, opened your gate, went inside your fence, teased the dog, and started screaming. Smith woke up from the nap, ran into your yard, and pulled the child away.

Instructions for Jones:

You are angry but concerned: Smith is negligent for sleeping while the child came unattended into your fenced yard through your closed gate and got hurt through no fault of yours. However, Smith has been a good neighbor and you want to preserve that relationship. Talk to Smith about what happened and how you want to preserve your relationship with Smith.

EXERCISE

Detecting Lies in Stories[56]

Background:

This exercise is based on a study in which 85 students were asked to tell stories about themselves to other students. Half of the student storytellers were instructed to tell true stories and half were instructed to tell false stories. The student listeners were instructed to record their assessments of each story. The study showed that a student listener's evaluation of the truth or falsity of a story correlated with the storyteller's ability to tell a well-structured story, and not with the actual truth or falsity of the story.

The Exercise:

This exercise requires a group of at least four people.

Identify three personal facts about yourself which no one else in the group knows about you (e.g., your hobbies, interests, accomplishments, travels, experiences at work or with your family, etc.) Two of the facts should be true and the third should be false.

Tell your three facts to the other members of the group who will each guess which fact is the lie. Debrief this experience in your group and talk about what exactly is a "lie" and ways in which you might be able to detect lies in a conflict story.

C. INTEGRATIVE PRINCIPLES

Rather than focusing solely on how to divide an existing "pie" that has a fixed value, parties employing the integrative strategy in negotiation and mediation first look for ways to create value to "expand the pie." The underlying principle is that both parties can be better off by looking jointly and creatively for ways to add value before they begin distributing value.

1. IN NEGOTIATION

While the Seven Elements of negotiation discussed in Chapter 1 provide a fuller, more comprehensive approach to integrative negotiation, at its most basic, there are three central steps to using the integrative approach: identifying interests, generating options, and evaluating options.

a. Identifying Interests

Negotiators using an integrative approach focus first on identifying interests. Key to identifying interests is distinguishing them from positions.

---

[56] See generally Stefan H. Krieger & Richard K. Neumann, Jr., *Essential Lawyering Skills: Teachers Manual* (2nd ed.) at 83. *See also* W. Lance Bennett & Martha S. Feldman, *Reconstructing Reality in the Courtroom: Justice and Judgment in American Culture* (1981) at 69–83.

Negotiators often begin by stating their positions. For example, a buyer might propose to a seller, "I won't pay more than $10,000 for the goods and I want them delivered in three weeks." This is the buyer's position. The seller doesn't yet know *why* that amount and the delivery time are important to the buyer. That *why* is the buyer's interest. Or as the seminal work *Getting to Yes* explains, "Interests motivate people; they are the silent movers behind the hubbub of positions."[57] Parties using positional bargaining don't get beyond their stated positions and end up arguing or haggling. By understanding and clarifying each other's interests, parties can begin to explore ways to create value for mutual gain.

In the example above, the seller might ask the buyer why delivery in three weeks is important to her and discover that she uses the goods in a product she sells and will lose money each week she is without the goods. The seller might be incurring costs each week for storing the goods and therefore has an interest in shipping them as soon as possible. Because both buyer and seller have a shared interest in the goods shipping quickly, they can begin to explore options that would be beneficial to both parties. Identifying interests allows the buyer and seller to begin to see areas for mutual gain.

Opportunities for mutual gain are found not only in shared interests. Often differences in interests are fertile ground for value creation. In BEYOND WINNING, authors Mnookin, Peppet, and Tulumello discuss five differences in interests between parties that can lead to mutual gain:[58]

1. **Different Resources**. If I have apples and you have oranges, and I need to make orange juice while you need to make apple pie, it may be useful for us to swap with each other.

2. **Different Relative Valuations**. Each of us has a combination of apples and oranges. We both like oranges, but I have an especially strong need for them to make orange juice, so I may be willing to give up enough apples to induce you to trade some of your oranges.

3. **Different Forecasts**. We both may have different ideas about what will transpire in the future. As an actor, you think our movie will be a huge success, and as a producer I think it will be more modest, so we arrange a contingency agreement for your salary that is lower upfront but provides bonuses as the movie hits certain box office benchmarks.

4. **Different Risk Preferences**. In buying a new computer I'm reluctant to take on the risk of it breaking within the first year, so I

----

[57] Roger Fisher, William Ury & Bruce Patton, GETTING TO YES (3rd ed.) 43 (New York: Penguin Books, 2011).

[58] Robert H. Mnookin, Scott Peppet & Andrew Tulumello, BEYOND WINNING, 14–15 (Cambridge: The Belknap Press of Harvard University Press, 2000).

buy an extended warranty that allows the computer company to absorb the risk, which it can do by pooling together revenues from other extended warranties it has sold to other buyers.

5. **Different Time Preferences**. You're selling a large set of books and you need to ship them right away to avoid storage costs. I am the buyer and I have access to cheap storage, but I don't feel strongly about when I receive the books. It may be beneficial for you to sell them to me at a lower price in exchange for me storing the books, which would enable you to ship them quickly and avoid your storage costs.

In all of these scenarios, differences in interests can lead to trades that create greater value (i.e., trades that can "expand the pie").

b.   Generating Options

After identifying interests, parties using an integrative approach then can begin generating options that satisfy their interests. The key to effective option generation is brainstorming. During a brainstorming session, parties should follow three ground rules: no such thing as a dumb idea (i.e., crazy ideas welcome); no evaluation or criticism; and quantity over quality. These rules allow parties to share ideas freely and can help produce a broader range of potential value-creating solutions. By welcoming and encouraging even ideas that seem wildly unrealistic, parties can spark creativity and help each other think more openly about options that satisfy both sides' interests. One especially helpful aspect of brainstorming is that it allows the parties to engage jointly in problem-solving. This can help avoid devolving into positional bargaining. Rather than pitting one person's ideas against another, the parties engage in a discussion free from evaluation and ownership that seeks to identify solutions that will create value and be mutually beneficial.

c.   Evaluating Options

Once the parties have generated a range of options through brainstorming, they can begin to evaluate which options best meet their interests. One effective way to evaluate options is to use objective criteria. These could be industry standards, comparisons to similarly situated deals (e.g., housing comparables), expert opinion, etc. If parties cannot come to an agreement on options that would satisfy both sides' interests, they can creatively explore procedural methods to decide which option they will select (e.g., flipping a coin, dividing value equally, taking turns choosing from a set of values, etc.).

While various negotiation contexts may call for various strategies, integrative negotiation is often most effective at producing agreements that create value and provide mutual gain for the negotiating parties.

2. IN MEDIATION

The central issue in an integrative mediation involves creative problem-solving that achieves a mutually acceptable joint solution to a mutually defined problem. By encouraging openness, collaboration, and creativity, the mediator helps parties work together to address each others' interests, expand resources, create value, and ultimately reach agreement. To do this, the mediator provides the parties with a structured process and guides them through the stages of integrative mediation:

- The parties create an agenda of the issues they need to discuss.
- The parties share information about their respective goals, objectives, and interests.
- Using the parties' interest-related information, the mediator helps the parties create, improve, and evaluate options that may meet their respective important interests.
- The parties select one option to which they both are willing to commit to agree.
- If the parties are unable to work together face-to-face, the mediator will work with each one separately in private caucuses and shuttle back and forth between them.

The effectiveness of the parties' relationship and the quality of their communication are important in integrative mediation. Whether or not the parties had a past relationship or will have an ongoing relationship, they have a problem-solving relationship during the mediation. Because the parties must work together to reach a mutually acceptable agreement, each party must share information about important interests and try to understand the other's important interests. Because interest-related information often is concealed by the parties' statements of initial positions or demands, the mediator may have to ask interest-related questions. For example, a mediator might say to a party who has made a firm monetary offer without providing an explanation of how she arrived at that figure or why she is insisting on it, "It sounds like you feel strongly about this amount. Help me understand how you arrived at that number."

Interests include positive and negative objectives, needs, desires, concerns, fears, aversions, and the like. They may be substantive or procedural in nature. Substantive interests include objective interests which are tangible, quantitative, and rational (e.g., a party's desire to get a sum of money), and subjective interests which are intangible, qualitative, and emotional (e.g., a party's desire to get an apology). Procedural interests are related to achieving an acceptable outcome in a manner that is perceived to be fair (e.g., by employing objective standards of legitimacy). Interests also may relate to third parties (e.g., family members, friends, or co-workers) who are affected by, but are not directly involved in, resolution of the parties' dispute.

Once information about the parties' respective interests is disclosed, the mediator seeks to understand how the parties prioritize their interests ranging from their "needs" (i.e., their most important interests that must be satisfied in an agreement) to their "wants" (i.e., their less important interests that they may be willing to concede or trade). This enables the mediator to help the parties create ways in which they might work together to satisfy their respective important interests. Something that is less important to one party may be very important to the other party, so there is an opportunity to create trades based on differences in the parties' preferences, resources, forecasts, or assessments of risk. Sometimes the parties are unable themselves to identify options for possible agreement and, therefore, the mediator may have to suggest some options for the parties to consider.

The mediator can help the parties select one option by employing criteria such as feasibility (i.e., will it work), objective legitimacy (e.g., appraisals or industry standards), perceived fairness, subjective satisfaction, and the parties' willingness and ability to commit to one option as their final agreement. The mediator also can help the parties improve an acceptable option so that it becomes more comprehensive and valuable by satisfying more of their respective interests. If necessary and appropriate, the mediator may help the parties informally document the terms of their agreement or help them draft a formal written contract to be signed by the parties memorializing the agreement.

3.   INTEGRATIVE SKILLS

The following are tools or skills that can be developed and employed in any negotiation or mediation, but tend to be especially relevant to the integrative approach, given its focus on collaboration and creative problem-solving.

The Toolbox:

- Lateral Thinking
    - Dominant idea
    - Reversal
    - Analogy
    - Random inputs
    - Component parts
    - Triage
    - Brainstorming
- The Six Thinking Hats

a.   Lateral Thinking[59]

It is difficult in the midst of conflict to think creatively. Fixed positions, strong emotions, and bruised egos get in the way. Author Edward DeBono invented the notion of "lateral thinking" as a strategy and set of techniques to help us creatively look at and think about problems from the side (i.e., laterally) rather than take them at face value (i.e., literally). Lateral thinking helps us approach situations in novel ways, look at problems from new perspectives, rearrange information using ingenious conceptual tools, and generate more options that may satisfy parties' important interests.

When faced with a problem, we tend to see it in terms of well-established patterns. For example, lawyers are trained to look at a personal injury case through the well-established patterns of the legal elements of the cause of action of negligence:

- Did the defendant owe a duty to protect the plaintiff from a latent hazard?
- Did the defendant breach that duty?
- Did the plaintiff sustain an injury?
- Was the defendant's breach of the duty the cause of the injury to the plaintiff?

To recover money damages, the plaintiff must prove each of the four legal elements of negligence. To prevent recovery of money damages, the defendant must disprove at least one of these four elements. The more lawyers look at the personal injury case, the more they focus on the existence or non-existence of these four elements. These well-established patterns tend to grow larger, more familiar, and therefore more limiting in the way they see the personal injury dispute.

Lateral thinking, by contrast, challenges our assumptions, conclusions, and other stereotyped ways of looking at things. For example, lateral thinking challenges our assumption of artificial pigeonholes of negligence law as rigid, true, and unchanging. There are other ways to look at a situation involving a personal injury, as any first-year law student is inclined to do before taking the torts course. To do this, lateral thinking involves innovation and creativity, i.e., building up something new, rather than analyzing something old; thinking about the present and the future, rather than focusing on the past.

The objective of lateral thinking is not to be right, but to be useful and effective. Our need to be right all the time blocks us from having or seeing new ideas (which often seem wrong until we test and improve them).

---

[59] See generally Edward DeBono, LATERAL THINKING: CREATIVITY STEP BY STEP (New York: Harper & Row, 1970).

Lateral thinking enables us to temporarily suspend our judgment, evaluation, and criticism of our own ideas and those offered by others.

Seven techniques that can help in employing lateral thinking involve using: (1) the dominant idea; (2) reversal; (3) analogy; (4) random inputs; (5) component parts; (6) triage; and (7) brainstorming.

One technique of lateral thinking involves changing the "**the dominant idea**," which is being used to look at a problem. The dominant idea resides not in the problem itself, but emerges from the way the problem is being looked at. For example, in thinking about the incidence of crime in a neighborhood, the dominant idea selected to look at the problem (and thereby describe the problem) may be the types of crime committed. This is not the only way to look at crime in a neighborhood. Alternatives to this particular dominant idea include: the kinds of victims; the socioeconomic causes of the crimes; the amount of crimes that were committed; the increasing (or diminishing) trends of crime; the ways to prevent crime; the economic impact of the crimes; etc. So, to use "the dominant idea" technique of lateral thinking, we identify the dominant idea that is currently being used to look at the problem, separate it from the details of the problem, replace it with a different dominant idea, and use it to re-analyze the problem.

"**Reversal**" involves thinking about a situation from the opposite direction. For example, the situation of a traffic cop directing traffic can be reversed into: traffic controlling the cop, or the cop disorganizing the flow of traffic. These may be wrong or silly ways of looking at the situation, but they allow us to escape from seeing only the original well-defined pattern. Reversal allows us to see a situation from new perspectives and thereby see new information, take new positions, etc.

"**Analogy**" is used to translate a situation into a simple, familiar, comparison-type story. For example, if the situation involves spreading gossip, this can be analogized to a snowball rolling downhill and getting bigger and bigger the farther it goes. The snowball analogy creates a new way of thinking about the gossip situation.

"**Random inputs**" which is a form of thinking by random analogy. This involves using some randomly selected idea, word, or object as a starting point to begin thinking about the original situation. For example, if the situation involves a housing shortage, the randomly selected word "noose" suggests tightening, suspension, loop, snare, etc., each of which may be a new way of thinking about the existing housing shortage.

"**Component parts**" are used to separate a familiar situation into individually named component parts which can be taken apart, looked at separately, and rearranged, i.e., moved around and combined in different ways not found in the initial situation. For example, in a personal injury case, instead of looking at "damages" as a single concept, we can look at the component parts of damages, which may include:

- General damages (i.e., pain and suffering)
- Special damages (i.e., out-of-pocket losses and costs)
  - Past damages
  - Future damages

The component parts of the special damages may include:

- Property damage
- Lost wages
- Medical expense:
  - Diagnostic
  - Treatment
  - Medication
- Disability:
  - Temporary vs. permanent
  - Partial vs. "whole man"
- Loss of activities:
  - Cognition
  - Household support
  - Hobbies
  - Consortium

"Triage" involves sorting components of a situation into three categories for efficient consideration. Examples of triage thinking include sorting things into:

- the familiar, the unfamiliar, and the useless;
- areas of agreement, disagreement, and irrelevance;
- willingness to say yes, no, and maybe; or
- things which seem at first glance to be plus, minus, and interesting.

"Brainstorming" involves working with others to invent new ideas or create new ways of solving a problem. Some suggestions for efficient brainstorming include:

- Take turns talking respectfully and listening attentively.
- State anything you can imagine to be helpful, no matter how wrong or silly it sounds.
- No judgment, evaluation, or criticism of an idea is permitted while brainstorming.
- Don't try to develop an idea in detail while brainstorming; a brief outline is sufficient.

- Write the parties' interests and suggested ideas on a white board or flip chart.
- Look for options that include both parties' interests.
- Look for possible low-cost/high-benefit trades.

b.   Six Thinking Hats[60]

Much of Western thought is based on critical, argumentative, and rhetorical models of thinking and communication developed by Aristotle and other philosophers in ancient Greece. Confrontational or adversarial thinking and speaking intensify conflicts, and limit our ability to perceive an issue from multiple perspectives. Critical thinking, analyses, critiques, and arguments are not sufficient by themselves to enable us to make good decisions. We also need to do other kinds of thinking and speaking about facts, feelings, creative problem-solving, positive and negative assessments, and the ways in which we can work together to do these things.

Edward DeBono has identified six distinct ways of thinking which focus on (1) facts, (2) emotions, (3) positive assessments, (4) negative assessments, (5) creativity, and (6) strategy. He describes these as six differently colored "thinking hats:"

White Hat Thinking is thinking about pure facts, data, and other information, without forming or giving interpretations or opinions:

> A request for White Hat Thinking is *"Just give me the facts, ma'am."* Western thinking, with its argumentative habits, prefers to give a conclusion first and then marshal facts to support the conclusion. In White Hat Thinking, we obtain and share usable, neutral information without coloring it with a point of view or conclusion.

Red Hat Thinking is thinking about our emotions and feelings without making or giving justifications or logical explanations for them:

> An example of Red Hat Thinking is *"I'm angry at you."* Emotions and feelings are strong and real. If not expressed directly, they color all other thinking. Red Hat Thinking makes emotions visible. Because emotions and feelings exist but are not "logical," we can state what they are, but we do not need to justify or explain them to ourselves or to others.

Yellow Hat Thinking is the positive assessment of value, benefits, and feasibility (which differs from being creative):

> A request for Yellow Hat Thinking is *"How can we improve this option?"* Yellow Hat Thinking presents the logical-positive: how to make something happen or make it work better. It is a deliberate search for

---

[60]   See generally Edward DeBono, Six Thinking Hats (Little, Brown and Company, 1985).

and vision of opportunities, benefits, and improvements. Yellow Hat Thinking should be used before Black Hat Thinking.

Black Hat Thinking is the negative assessment of risks, dangers, costs, and infeasibility (but it is not argumentation):

> An example of Black Hat Thinking is *"This option is not feasible because it costs more than we have budgeted."* Black Hat Thinking presents the logical-negative: why something will not work. This kind of thinking challenges assumptions, conclusions, and predictions. It also points out risks, dangers, and potential problems, but it is *not* argument.

Green Hat Thinking is creative thinking, "lateral" thinking, and thinking "outside the box:"

> An example of Green Hat Thinking is *"Rather than arguing about who was right and who was wrong, let's talk about ways we can resolve this now."* Green Hat Thinking jumps over obstacles and cuts across patterns to create new ideas. It is the willingness to visualize multiple options that might work and might be acceptable. It is the forward-looking "eureka" of a paradigm shift.

Blue Hat Thinking is controlled thinking which sets the focus, defines the problem, and frames the strategy:

> An example of Blue Hat Thinking is *"Let's make an agenda, discuss our interests, create some options, evaluate the ones that work, and then make a choice."* Blue Hat Thinking is thinking about thinking. It plans our thinking. It tells us how to organize thinking into an appropriate sequence. It tells us which thinking hat is the most suitable to use, which to use first, and when to switch hats.

Most conversation in a high-conflict situation is an argumentative muddle of Black Hat evaluation, White Hat facts, and unexpressed Red Hat emotions lurking in the background: for example, *"I will never pay alimony to you. [This is a statement of a White Hat fact.] No court would ever make me do that. [This is Black Hat thinking.]" [Unexpressed, but underlying everything is the Red Hat emotion, "I am furious at you because you betrayed and humiliated me when you had an affair with my best friend."]* The six kinds of thinking discussed by DeBono are conceptual tools that can be used to sort through the muddle of a difficult deal or dispute. These tools work because they provide a focused, systematic, and sequenced way of thinking and talking.

DeBono believes that the greatest impediments to effective thinking are complexity and rigidity. Most people in conflict deal with too many things simultaneously and they try to assess all aspects of a problem at once. This can create a muddle. To remain rigidly focused on a complex problem also deters people from exploring facts, feelings, creative ideas, and ways to work together. DeBono's thinking hats simplify complexity by focusing thinking on one distinct aspect of a problem at a time. They bypass rigidity by using all six thinking hats to examine a problem in multiple ways, taking into account everyone's various perspectives and input. When each person sequentially looks at and talks about the same thing at the same time (e.g., first about facts, then about emotions, then about brainstorming, etc.), they are engaging in what DeBono calls "parallel thinking" which reduces complexity and rigidity.

Because most people are unfamiliar with DeBono's six thinking hats, negotiators and mediators may choose to use these tools without mentioning their color names. Instead, negotiators and mediators can use the six thinking hats as background strategies or mental checklists for planning and having specific kinds of conversations or asking specific kinds of questions. By invisibly using these tools in this manner, negotiators and mediators can:

- develop more accurate and more comprehensive information about issues, interests, emotions, and concerns;
- engage in brainstorming that generates more creative options;
- improve and evaluate options; and
- make appropriate decisions about committing to one option as the final agreement.

The following table describes and contrasts the six thinking hats, gives examples of how each can be used, and summarizes their distinct purposes:

Table Comparing Edward de Bono's "Six Thinking Hats"

White-Hat Thinking (deals with information, facts, and data, but without criticism or judgment): • What information do we have? • What information do we need? • Where can we get more information? White-Hat Thinking deals with neutral and objective facts and figures, free from interpretation or opinion. If conflicting facts are suggested, they are listed without argument or criticism. This marshals a mutual database of potentially relevant information.	**Red-Hat Thinking** (deals with emotions, but without explanation or justification of why they exist): • Tell me what you feel at this moment. • I'll describe how I feel about this issue. Red-Hat Thinking allows us to express our feelings, emotions, hunches, and intuitions without any need to explain or justify them. It is important to resist the impulse or demand to justify our feelings, because their existence, validity, and influence in conflict are not based on whether they are logical or appropriate.
Yellow-Hat Thinking (deals with positive assessments, e.g., of how and why things work): • What are positive implications of the options? • What are the benefits if we choose this option? • Which is the best option now available to us? Yellow-Hat Thinking is concerned with positive assessments, ranging from logical and practical ideas to our dreams, visions, and hopes for the future. It probes and explores for value and benefit, and seeks to find rational support for proposed ideas.	**Black-Hat Thinking** (deals with negative assessments, e.g., of how and why things don't work): • How does this fail to satisfy our interests? • What are the difficulties in implementing this? • Why does this option violate existing law? Black-Hat Thinking legitimizes the value and importance of caution and risk assessment. It relieves us of the burden of having to be fair-minded and having to address at the same time both the positive and negative implications of available options.
Green-Hat Thinking (deals with creativity, brainstorming, and new perspectives): • What are ways we might solve this problem? • How might we land a man on Mars tomorrow? • What if I bolt roller-skate wheels on luggage? Green-Hat Thinking involves the deliberate creation of new ideas and new approaches to problem solving. It is an intentional and focused effort to generate options and facilitate change. It places value on ridiculous and unworkable ideas that exist outside our usual thinking patterns, because that may move us outside our normal habits of perception to take a new perspective.	**Blue-Hat Thinking** (deals with organizing and directing relevant strategies of productive thinking): • What is the problem we are trying to solve? • What kinds of thinking will help us solve it? • What should we do first, second, third, etc.? Blue-Hat Thinking defines a problem; analyzes the situation; determines the appropriate strategy to use for solving the problem; identifies priorities, resources, and constraints; directs implementation of the strategy; and monitors and measures progress. Used at the end of problem solving, Blue-Hat thinking summarizes, articulates, and explains our conclusions to others.

Using the "Six Thinking Hats" to Resolve a Conflict

1.   IDENTIFY MUDDLED THINKING: Most thinking in a conflict is an argumentative muddle of Black Hat and White Hat Thinking, with unexpressed Red Hat emotions in the background.

2. TRIAGE THE CONFLICT: Blue Hat Thinking maps out the areas of agreement, the areas of disagreement, and the areas of irrelevance for the parties in the conflict.

3. VISUALIZE FEELINGS: Red Hat Thinking sees and acknowledges the parties' emotions and invites and permits their expression without requiring an explanation or justification.

4. GET RELEVANT INFORMATION: White Hat Thinking obtains and shares neutral information useful to the parties. It also seeks prior "state of the art" solutions of similar conflicts.

5. SEEK SUGGESTIONS; MAKE PROPOSALS: Green Hat Thinking seeks ways to make something happen (i.e., possible solutions) which have value and benefit for the parties in the conflict.

6. BRAINSTORM POSSIBLE SOLUTIONS: Engage in constructive thinking about possible solutions by using factual White Hat, positive Yellow Hat, and creative Green Hat Thinking.

7. TRIAGE POSSIBLE SOLUTIONS: Blue Hat Thinking organizes proposals into those requiring individual consideration, those requiring joint consideration, and those that just get noted.

8. IDENTIFY LIKELY SOLUTIONS: Yellow Hat Thinking identifies and improves those proposals that seem to have more value and benefit for the parties in the conflict.

9. ELIMINATE UNLIKELY SOLUTIONS: Black Hat Thinking identifies those proposals that are impossible, unusable, too expensive, or unacceptable. Those proposals are given no further consideration.

10. CHOOSE THE SOLUTION: Red Hat Thinking expresses the parties' feelings about the proposals. Yellow Hat and Black Hat Thinking identify the proposal that best satisfies the parties' goals, objectives, and interests.

11. IMPROVE THE SOLUTION:[61] Yellow Hat Thinking and Green Hat Thinking add "bells and whistles," strengthen any weaknesses, and fix any remaining problems in the chosen solution.

12. IMPLEMENT THE SOLUTION: Blue Hat Thinking reviews what the parties have accomplished and creates a plan to implement their solution. This may involve getting necessary third-party commitment and reducing the parties' agreement to writing.

---

[61] After having conducted hundreds of mediations, we have observed that many lawyers accept the first feasible solution to a problem without spending additional time and effort figuring out how to improve it by "expanding the pie" and making it more attractive or more valuable to both parties. By contrast, business people seem to do this more often.

EXERCISE

Using the "Six Thinking Hats" to Analyze a
High–Conflict Conversation

Most high-conflict conversation is an argumentative muddle of Black Hat and White Hat Thinking, with unexpressed Red Hat emotions in the background. Identify a high-conflict conversation you have had with someone who is important to you. (The greater the conflict and the more important the person is to you, the better this example is to analyze.)

Analyze the conversation using the "Six Thinking Hats" to see which different ways of thinking you used in this conversation and how you used them. Are there other Thinking Hats you could have used in the conversation (or used in different ways) that would have helped improve the quality or the outcome of the conversation?

White Hat Thinking: pure facts and information (*without* interpretations or opinions):

Red Hat Thinking: actual emotions and feelings (*without* justifications or explanations):

Yellow Hat Thinking: positive assessment of possible value, benefits, feasibility, etc.:

Black Hat Thinking: negative assessment of risks, dangers, costs, etc. (*without* arguments):

Green Hat Thinking: brainstorming and creative thinking about new possibilities:

Blue Hat Thinking: controlled thinking about what type of thinking to use and when:

EXERCISE

A "Conflict Stories" Conversation in Integrative Negotiation

This exercise illustrates what can happen in a conflict conversation in which the parties are trying to create a mutual-gains resolution of a problem that also preserves their relationship.

You and a partner should assume fictional names: one of you is "Smith" and the other is "Jones." Smith should read the "Confidential Information for Smith" on the following page. Jones should read the "Confidential Information for Jones" on the second page following this one.

Conduct your conversation for about five minutes. After the conversation, discuss with your partner what you experienced.

"The Bitten Child" Conversation in
Integrative Negotiation

Confidential Information for Smith

Background facts for Smith:

Your neighbor Jones has a large dog in the front yard, which is fenced but has an unlocked gate. You have complained several times to your neighbor about keeping such a large dog in an unlocked yard.

You have a three-year-old child. You were home alone with your child and you took a nap on the couch. While you were asleep, your child opened the back door of your house, went next door, opened the unlocked gate, went inside the fence, teased the dog, and was bitten in the face. You heard your child's screams, ran next door, and took your child to the hospital, where your child received a dozen stitches. Fortunately, it does not appear that there will be permanent, noticeable scarring from the dog bites.

Instructions for Smith:

You want to resolve the problem so that it never happens again in the future. You are willing to take responsibility for falling asleep when your child went into Jones' yard. You want to preserve your relationship with Jones who has been a good neighbor. You also would like Jones to reimburse you for the emergency room co-payment amount of $75.00. Talk to Jones about how to solve this problem in a way that also preserves your relationship.

"The Negligent Parent" Conversation in Integrative Negotiation

Confidential Information for Jones

Background facts for Jones:

You have a large but gentle dog in your front yard, which is fenced with a closed but unlocked gate. Your neighbor Smith has a three-year-old child who has come unattended into your yard several times to play with your dog. You have been concerned that the child could be bitten if it played too rough with your dog.

Smith was home alone with the child. Instead of supervising the child, Smith took a nap. While Smith slept, Smith's child got out of the house, opened your gate, went inside your fence, played with the dog, and was bitten in the face. Smith woke up from the nap, ran into your yard, pulled the child away, and took the child to the hospital for stitches.

Instructions for Jones:

You want to resolve this problem so that it will never happen again in the future. You are willing to put a lock on the gate. You are worried that the child will have permanent scarring. You are worried that Smith will report your dog to Animal Control. You are willing to compensate Smith for any out-of-pocket expense required at the hospital. Talk to Smith about solving the problem in a way that preserves your relationship.

D. DISTRIBUTIVE PRINCIPLES

The distributive strategy in negotiation and mediation is about dividing up value. Whether parties have spent time creating value and "expanding the pie," or they are simply dividing up a fixed amount, the distributive approach is the method through which parties claim value.

1. IN NEGOTIATION

A distributive negotiation generally works in the following way. Each party has a negotiating range with a starting point, a target, and a stopping point:

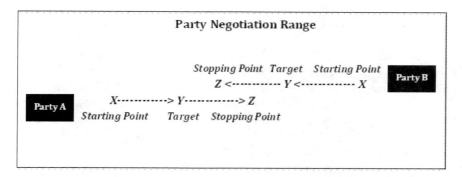

Neither party discloses its target or stopping point to the other. The parties customarily expect that there will be some back-and-forth bargaining after they disclose their respective starting points. Typically, one party makes an offer and the other makes a counteroffer and so on, until they reach an agreement or impasse. Sometimes the initial offer and subsequent counteroffers are accompanied with a statement of (purported) legitimacy that explains or justifies the offer (e.g., "I will pay $X for your widget, because that price was advertised in today's newspaper by another seller").

The sequence of offer and counteroffers is very important. It is supposed to move the bargaining exchange along by influencing the parties to adjust their positions. Each move by a party narrows the negotiation range between the parties. The parties' bargaining behavior thereby funnels the negotiation into a zone of potential agreement ("ZOPA"). This zone in which the parties' offers and counteroffers trend toward their stopping points is where they potentially can reach a deal. If the stopping points do overlap in the ZOPA, a deal is possible. If the stopping points do not overlap, a deal is impossible unless one or both parties readjust their stopping points.

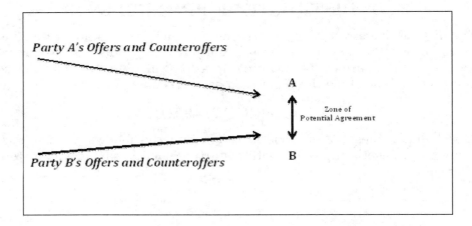

Each offer and counteroffer sends "signals" back and forth about the parties' target points and stopping points. For example, if Party A's starting offer is too far away from its target point, the starting offer may appear foolish or unreasonable to Party B, who may decide to break off negotiations. During a distributive negotiation, each party will likely be able to infer the other's target point because parties typically are willing to give up the difference between their starting points and their target points, i.e., they are willing to move closer and closer to their respective target points during the bargaining process. As a means of justifying an offer, parties often will look to and maybe invoke objective criteria such as industry standards, expert opinion, current comparable trends, historical patterns, etc. Objective criteria can help provide legitimacy to the distributive process.

a. The Distinction Between Positional Bargaining and Distributive Negotiation

Traditionally, positional bargaining has been used synonymously with distributive negotiation in negotiation literature. By contrast, we are positing that they are actually two distinct things. Distributive negotiation is an economically rational strategy that a party can employ to divide up value. It consists of parties exchanging offers back and forth, with each conceding some movement until an agreement is reached. Sometimes parties employ positional bargaining tactics in distributive negotiation, which might include manipulation, deception, intimidation, etc., but these tactics are not a defining characteristic of distributive negotiation.

In fact, the exchange of offers and counteroffers in distributive negotiation is theoretically driven by each party's consideration of relevant applicable legitimacy information and the strength or weakness of her BATNA, which is the rational basis for distributive negotiation. We believe that when parties in distributive negotiation are not aware of (and therefore cannot use) legitimacy information and their BATNAs to negotiate, they tend to default into merely using positional bargaining behaviors, simply because they have no economically rational basis for conducting effective distributive negotiation.

Attempting to "anchor" high or low with an aggressive but rational opening offer or counteroffer in distributive negotiation is not the same as an aggressive but irrational opening offer or counteroffer in positional bargaining that is based in manipulation, deception, intimidation, etc., even though they may appear from the outside to be similar behaviors. Because they lack rationality, we categorize positional bargaining behaviors as a form of performative negotiation. Chapter 4 of this book discusses in detail how to deal with the "difficult tactics" commonly found in positional bargaining.

The table below provides a summary of distributive negotiation concepts:

Concept	Explanation
Legitimacy	Objective standards of fairness (e.g., market value, precedents, industry standards) and fair procedures (e.g., appraisals, bidding, split-the-difference).
Alternatives	The range of possible things a party can do outside the negotiation without having the other negotiator's agreement.
BATNA	The Best Alternative to a Negotiated Agreement (BATNA) is the alternative a party will take, if no agreement is reached in the negotiation.
Stopping point	Also known as "reservation value." The amount where a party is indifferent between reaching agreement and taking the BATNA.
ZOPA	The Zone of Potential Agreement is the apparent range created by the parties' stopping points. It conceals an overlap or an actual gap (impasse).
Target	Translation of standards of legitimacy and a party's interests, strategy, and tactics into an amount in the negotiation the party wants to achieve.
Starting point	A party's initial offers should be credible and should incentivize the other party to continue negotiating.

Concept	Explanation
Negotiating range	The parties' initial offers establish their overall negotiating range. As the parties narrow this gap by movements over time, they generate a time-funnel toward the ZOPA.
Protocol	Reasonable and customary expectations about the parties' pattern of counteroffers that funnel the parties' negotiation toward the ZOPA.
Signaling	"Information" about intentions, including direct communication between the parties and indirect inferences from the parties' patterns of counteroffers.

2. IN MEDIATION

Many legal disputes are distributive situations involving the exchange of money for some kind of legal consideration. In negotiating a personal injury case, for example, the parties negotiate about how much money the defendant will pay and how little money the plaintiff will accept, in exchange for a formal written release of the defendant's liability and dismissal of the plaintiff's lawsuit with prejudice (i.e., so that it can never be filed again). Distributive disputes pose unique challenges for a mediator, because all Seven Elements of negotiation complicate the mediation:

1. The parties' **relationship** often is polarized as a result of ineffective pre-mediation bargaining, so the parties (or their lawyers) are frustrated or angry with one another at the beginning of the mediation.

2. The **communication** between the parties (or their lawyers) often involves using doubt-creating behaviors of manipulation or deception, such as bluffs, exaggerations, unrealistic offers, take-it-or-leave-it demands, threats of walking out and going to trial, etc.

3. Parties rarely disclose their underlying **interests** or concerns in distributive mediation (not even to the mediator in caucus), so there is very little known positive movement-motivation information.

4. The parties' **options** are typically the exchange of offers of countervailing amounts of money, often starting with an aggressive initial offer and equally aggressive counteroffer.

5. The parties (or their lawyers) either do not have or cannot agree on an applicable objective standard of **legitimacy** to use to determine the settlement value of their dispute.

6. A party's **alternative** in distributive mediation of a legal dispute typically is going to court if the dispute is not settled. In distributive mediation, due to the advocate's bias, parties often inflate the strength of their own BATNA and discount the strength of the other party's BATNA.

7. Before they are able to make a **commitment** about settlement, parties in distributive mediation often need a mediator's evaluation of the strengths and weaknesses of their respective BATNAs, or the mediator's opinion about the settlement value of the dispute or the likely outcome if the dispute were tried in court. Because the parties typically do not know the other side's underlying interests, the motivation behind each side's commitment is not visible.

To overcome these unique challenges, the mediator in distributive mediation must in effect be a negotiation coach for the parties and help improve the quality of their relationship and communication during the mediation, encourage them to share information about their underlying interests, monitor and increase the effectiveness of their exchange of offers and counteroffers, and incentivize their movement toward settlement. To do this, the distributive mediator in a legal dispute must:

- manage the parties' unproductive venting of negative emotions that unnecessarily polarize the parties' relationship and degrade their communication during the mediation;

- typically use the caucus process in mediation to meet privately with one party at a time to attempt to get interest-related information and to do risk analysis;

- meet first in caucus with the party who is expected to make the first offer in mediation or the next counteroffer to an existing pre-mediation offer;

- recommend to a party a specific move in making a counteroffer, or counsel the party how a particular move is likely to be received by the other party as unhelpful;

- avoid conveying polarizing or offensive language that one party expresses in caucus about the other party;

- encourage the parties to engage in realistic cost-benefit-risk-analysis and create a projected budget of the estimated cost of going forward, if the case is not settled in mediation, including the cost of completing discovery, conducting motion practice, preparing for trial, and trying the case in court; and

- give evaluations or recommend end-game tactics that enable the parties to save face as they move past their pre-planned stopping points to reach a feasible settlement.

Because of these unique requirements of distributive mediation, lawyers often select mediators who have expertise in the subject matter of the dispute and who are willing to be evaluative. Evaluative mediators typically are very experienced trial lawyers or former judges who are willing to give opinions about the strengths and weaknesses of the parties' BATNAs, the settlement value of a case, or the likely outcome of a dispute at trial if it is not settled in mediation. Evaluative mediation typically occurs when a distributive mediation appears headed for impasse and the parties' lawyers ask the mediator to give an expert opinion about the dispute's risks, value, or likely outcome in court.

One particularly challenging kind of distributive mediation involves an injured plaintiff and multiple defendants who have varying amounts of legal responsibility for the plaintiff's harm. Often it is easy for the defendants to agree on an amount that should be offered to the plaintiff as fair compensation for her injuries. However, it is difficult almost to the point of impossibility for the defendants to agree among themselves how much each defendant should contribute to fund a fair settlement offer. Each defendant thinks the other defendants are more responsible and therefore should contribute more to fund the settlement offer, which leads to impasse. To try to overcome such an impasse, the distributive mediator typically has to caucus separately with each defendant or with sub-groups of defendants. Sophisticated defendants in this kind of mediation often choose a mediator who is capable and willing to engage in credible evaluative and directive interventions when impasse inevitably occurs during the mediation.

3. DISTRIBUTIVE SKILLS

The following are tools or skills that can be developed and employed in any negotiation or mediation, but tend to be especially relevant to the distributive approach, given its focus on dividing value among parties.

The Toolbox:

- Anchoring
- Cost–Benefit Analysis: Consequences Table
- Dealing with Uncertainty
    - Risk Profiles
    - Decision Trees
- Fair and Effective Process

a. Anchoring

Whether to throw out the first number in a negotiation can be a difficult strategic decision. Without sufficient knowledge of what the other party is willing to pay (or accept), you risk beginning with an offer that may leave a significant amount of money on the table. Lax and Sebenius relate the experience of Thomas Edison, who, after inventing a type of stock ticker, was approached by a large company to buy it. Edison had calculated that the time and effort he spent inventing the device was worth $5,000. However, this seemed like such a large sum that he couldn't bring himself to ask for it up front, and instead, asked the company to make the first offer. One can imagine Edison's surprise, when the company offered $40,000. Of course, Edison accepted.[62] By allowing the other side to make an offer first, Edison avoided leaving $35,000 on the table. While Edison's transaction provides a cautionary tale about initial offers, Lax and Sebenius advise that unless you are completely unaware of the other party's general price range, it is better to throw out the first number because of the so-called "anchoring effect."

The anchoring effect is a well-established psychological phenomenon that shows how a number can influence the bargaining range and, ultimately, the agreed-upon price in a negotiation. Kahneman explains the anchoring effect as follows:

> It occurs when people consider a particular value for an unknown quantity before estimating that quantity. What happens is one of the most reliable and robust results of experimental psychology: the estimates stay close to the number that people considered—hence the image of an anchor. If you are asked whether Gandhi was more than 114 years old when he died you will end up with a much higher estimate of his age at death than you would if the anchoring question referred to death at 35. If you consider how much you should pay for a house, you will be influenced by the asking price. The same house will appear more valuable if its listing price is high than if it is low, even if you are determined to resist the influence of this number.[63]

A party that starts with the first number can strategically anchor the negotiation at a high or low number. As Lax and Sebenius point out, "when an anchor is introduced into a negotiation, it can shift perceptions of the ZOPA in its direction, thereby increasing the odds that any final agreement will drift toward the anchor."[64] While this idea might lead one to conclude "when it comes to initial offers, the higher the better," Lax and Sebenius caution that this works only to a point; if the number is too extreme, you risk losing credibility and appearing unreasonable.[65] They provide a few recommendations for effective anchoring:

---

[62] David A. Lax & James K. Sebenius, 3D NEGOTIATION at 187 (Cambridge: Harvard Business School Press, 2006).

[63] Daniel Kahneman, THINKING, FAST AND SLOW at 119–120 (New York: Farrar, Straus, and Giroux, 2011).

[64] Lax & Sebenius, *supra* note 63 at 189.

[65] *Id.* at 190.

1. *Justify your proposal.*[66] Instead of just throwing out a number, a
    party should provide reasons for the amount she has offered. Re-
    search has demonstrated that people are more likely to accept an
    offer if it is tied to some kind of principled explanation, so a party
    who starts with a number, especially if he knows it is likely con-
    sidered to be extreme by the other party, should be prepared to
    explain why that number makes sense or what criteria justify it.

2. *Use "flexible but extreme offers."*[67] To avoid the risks of starting
    with an extreme *firm* offer, a party can utilize a lower-risk strate-
    gy by employing an extreme *flexible* offer. Rather than informing
    the other party you are willing to pay only a certain amount, you
    can frame the offer in a way that suggests your willingness to en-
    tertain other amounts if circumstances change. "We understand
    from what you've described in our conversations that there is sub-
    stantial hidden value in the company. We haven't yet been able to
    evaluate your arguments about the company's value. So, we'll of-
    fer you $11 million based on what we know today, but are open to
    modifying that offer if we're persuaded about the additional value
    you've described."[68] The flexibility displayed here helps decrease
    the chances the seller would just walk away because she is offend-
    ed or put-off by an extremely low number.

3. *Use "non-offer offers."*[69] Rather than making a specific offer, a
    party would introduce relevant numbers that provide an
    anchoring effect. For example, in a negotiation for the price of a
    shipment of goods, a party could suggest that other shipping
    companies have completed similar orders for $2,000 (an extremely
    low offer). Similarly, a seller in a business transaction could cite
    past transactions as guiding precedent without giving a specific
    offer: "We've done similar transactions for 30% above the cost of
    goods."

Because anchors can be a powerful tool in negotiation, it is important to
know not only how to employ anchors effectively as an offensive tool but
how to respond defensively if the other party has tried to anchor you with
an extreme number. Lax and Sebenius recommend ruling out of
consideration such offers firmly and clearly. A party may consider making
an equally extreme counteroffer or even walking away. Depending on the
context, humor or nonverbal cues also can be ways to signal that the offer
is unacceptable.[70]

---

[66] *Id.* at 190.
[67] Id. at 191–192.
[68] *Id.* at 191.
[69] *Id.* at 191–192.
[70] *Id.* at 194–196.

In addition to communicating to the other party that their offer is no-where near acceptable, a party can also shift the focus of the negotiation. One way to do this is by shifting the metric.[71] If a party is proposing a number based on certain criteria, you can un-anchor by dismissing those criteria and proposing a new set of criteria. For example, if a house seller starts with an extremely high number based on the square footage of the house, a buyer could counter by dismissing square footage as an im-portant factor to her and instead use criteria such as the long driving time to work and the lack of proximity to quality schools. Using these metrics, the buyer could reset the anchor in a way more favorable to her by emphasizing that other houses she has looked at are closer to work and near to better schools.

As a cautionary note about the purported benefits of anchoring, and based on having watched hundreds of pairs of lawyers make and respond to opening offers in mediation, our observation is that experienced, well-prepared negotiators generally are not affected by the anchoring phenom-enon.

<u>Suggestions for Making or Responding to Offers in Distributive Negotia-tion</u>

1. Be well-prepared (e.g., use the Seven Elements of negotiation as a preparation checklist).

2. Prepare a rational negotiating range (with starting point, target, and stopping point) for distributive negotiation.

3. Generally, your starting point must be credible or you risk being perceived as:
   • not knowing what you are doing, or
   • not negotiating in good faith.

4. Prepare a script for your opening lines which:
   • acknowledges both parties' perspectives, and
   • expresses your commitment to negotiate for a mutually fair agreement.

5. Prepare an agenda of issues to be negotiated. Ask the other nego-tiator whether there are other issues that should be added to the agenda. If possible, write the issues on a whiteboard or flip chart.

6. Generally, make the first offer unless the other negotiator has more information. Have and be prepared to give a principled ex-planation of your offer, e.g., "We just did a similar deal for $X."

7. If the other negotiator goes first, remember the anchoring as-sumption, i.e., the other negotiator assumes that her high (or low) opening offer will anchor your expectations that the final agree-

---

[71] *Id.* at 195.

ment will be in a range closer to her opening number. Be prepared to rebut her anchoring assumption.

8. If you go second, remember the "shaping" phenomenon, i.e., that a response often is shaped by the logic and amount of the opening offer. When you go second, you have a choice to either:

   • acknowledge and assess the opening remarks in making your response, or

   • ignore the opening remarks and make your own offer, as if you were going first.

9. Do not make an offer that is a range of numbers (e.g., "I am willing to pay between $15,000 and $20,000). By making such an offer, you have informed the other negotiator that you will pay as much as $20,000.

10. Generally, do not agree *seriatim* to individual issues in a multi-issue negotiation. Analyze the whole package of negotiated issues before committing to a global agreement.

11. If the other negotiator makes a non-negotiable offer, you have a number of choices in deciding how to respond:

   • Ignore the non-negotiable offer and make a counteroffer.

   • Share legitimacy information or disclose your BATNA, if they are strong, to critique the non-negotiable offer, and then make a counteroffer.

   • Accept the non-negotiable offer if it is within your negotiating range.

   • Ask questions to understand the basis of the offer and why it is not negotiable, before you decide whether to respond with a counteroffer.

   • Reject the non-negotiable offer and explain why you rejected it (e.g., it exceeds the relevant legitimacy standard or it exceeds your BATNA). Then either make a counteroffer or break off negotiations.

   • Generally speaking, do not demand that the party who made a non-negotiable offer must make another, more reasonable offer before you will respond with a counteroffer. This violates the customary bargaining protocol that parties are expected to take turns making and responding to offers. Once the non-negotiable offer is made, it is your turn to respond.

b.   Cost–Benefit–Risk Analysis: Using a Consequences Table

Negotiation and mediation always involve making decisions. What should I say? How should I react? Should I accept her offer?

While different situations involve different types of decisions (intuition, heuristics, random choice, etc.), negotiators and mediators are frequently involved in making analytical decisions—i.e., decisions that are conducive to cost-benefit-risk analysis, where a party can weigh the pros and cons, risks and rewards, and compare the relative advantage of choosing one option over another. However, despite the prevalence of analytical decision-making opportunities, many negotiators and mediators fail to utilize analytical tools that could assist them in guiding themselves, their clients, or the disputing parties to a good decision. One particularly effective tool in this regard is the consequences table.

Hammond, Keeney, and Raiffa describe how to construct and use a consequences table.[72] The first step is to properly identify the problem. Often people frame problems inappropriately, which leads them to grapple with the wrong decision.[73] For example, is the problem really about which car I should buy, or should it be about whether I need to buy a car at all? Is it about accepting a job at Firm A or Firm B, or is it about whether I should be looking at private sector or public sector jobs?

After properly identifying the problem, we need to ascertain our objectives.[74] We can discover our objectives by exploring our interests and identifying what is most important to us. Frequently, objectives are disguised as options. For example, we might think that our objective is to earn a certain amount of money each year. But as we probe more deeply into what is driving that concern, we realize that our desired annual salary is masking a series of more specific interests, such as the type of home we would like to live in, traveling we'd like to do, and other lifestyle issues.

Next we should create what the authors call "alternatives" (synonymous with the Harvard Negotiation Project's term "options," which we use in this book). We can make decisions that better satisfy our objectives if we have developed strong options. Some ways to create options include looking over our objectives and thinking creatively about ways we could meet them; challenging constraints; consulting with others; and setting high aspirations.[75]

Following the creation of options, we should then think through the consequences of each option. The authors recommend thinking of yourself at some future date as if you had chosen a particular option, and then describing in detail the consequences of that choice.[76]

---

[72] John S. Hammond, Ralph L. Keeney & Howard Raiffa, SMART CHOICES at 63–78 (New York: Broadway Books, 2002).

[73] *Id.* at 15–28.

[74] *Id.* at 29–43.

[75] *Id.* at 45–62.

[76] *Id.* at 63–68.

After objectives, options, and consequences have been identified, we can proceed to evaluate our options by using a consequences table. Using a paper or computer spreadsheet, list the objectives in a column along the left side of the paper, and then list the options along the top. With this matrix, write the consequence of each option as it matches up a corresponding objective. The following is a sample consequences table for a married couple with two school-age children trying to decide among three different cities to which they might move.[77]

Objectives	Options		
	City A	*City B*	*City C*
Cost of living	High	Medium	Low
Public transportation	Extensive	Limited	Moderate
Weather	Poor	Great	Great
Quality of schools	Medium	Poor	Excellent
Bike paths	Moderate	Many	Many
Safety	High crime	Moderate crime	Low crime

With the information laid out in the consequences table, the couple can easily see that City C, with its low cost of living, decent public transportation, high quality schools, etc., meets their objectives much better than the other two. By forcing ourselves to think through our objectives, create options, and then list out (and, where possible, quantify) our consequences, we can create a systematic method for comparing options. Rather than agonizing aimlessly over options that can seem completely muddled conceptually, the consequences table allows us to see our options laid out clearly against each other, enabling us to select more easily the option that best meets our objectives.

It is possible to quantify the comparison of options in a consequences table by:

1) weighting the relative importance of the objectives one to another, e.g., if "Cost of living" is twice as important as "Public transportation," then "Cost of living" gets a weighting factor of 2.0, and "Public transportation" gets a weighting factor of 1.0;

2) assigning a numerical range of how well or how poorly an option satisfies an objective, e.g., on a range from 0 to 3, "Cost of living" in City A receives a score of 1, whereas "Cost of living" in City B

---

[77] See generally SMART CHOICES, *supra* note 73 at 69.

receives a score of 2, and "Cost of living" in City C receives a score of 3;

3) then multiplying each option's score by each objective's weighting factor, e.g., "Cost of living" in City A receives a weighted score of 2, whereas "Cost of living" in City B receives a weighted score of 4, and "Cost of living" in City C receives a weighted score of 6; and

4) finally adding up the total scores of each option and comparing the columns' totals one to another (i.e., the option with the highest score satisfies your objectives more than do the other options).

In quantifying a consequences table, it is useful to explain to a friend why you chose a particular weighting factor for an objective and how you assigned a particular score to an option.

c. Dealing with Uncertainty: Using Risk Profiles and Decision Trees

Many decisions involve some level of uncertainty. We cannot always know what consequences will follow from our decisions: sometimes good decisions have bad consequences, and sometimes bad decisions have good consequences. For example, in deciding whether to wear a seatbelt, I might be aware of data that show there is a 95% chance that a seatbelt protects me from injury in a car accident and a 5% chance that wearing the seatbelt will cause worse injuries. After considering the odds, I decide to wear the seatbelt and then become involved in a car accident in which my injuries are more severe because I wore the seatbelt. This doesn't mean that wearing the seatbelt was a bad decision, only that the consequence in this instance was bad. Because of uncertainty, we cannot always know what consequences will follow from our decisions; however, we can take steps to deal with uncertainty and make it more likely that we make smart choices.

One way to help simplify decisions involving uncertainty is to create a risk profile.[78] Hammond, Keeney, and Raiffa explain this as a four-step process: (1) identify the key uncertainties; (2) define outcomes; (3) assign chances; and (4) describe the consequences of each outcome.[79] To demonstrate how this works, consider the example of Lora, a graphic designer who has been offered a one-year position at a prestigious design firm. The firm has told her that if things go well, they may renew her contract for another year, or potentially offer her a long-term contract. Ideally, she'd be interested in a long-term contract with the firm, and a two-year stint with the firm would be long enough to give her terrific experience that would be beneficial as she seeks employment when the contract expires. Her concern is that if the contract is not renewed,

---

[78] *Id.* at 108.

[79] *Id.* at 108.

spending only one year at the firm would reflect badly on others' perception of her competence. Also, accepting the position would require her to move to a different city, and because the firm is the only one of its kind in that city, she'd have to move to yet another city to find work if the contract is not renewed. Therefore, she devises the following risk profile:[80]

Risk Profile for Accepting a Short–Term Position

Uncertainty: Whether the contract will be renewed.

Outcome	Chance	Consequences
No renewal	Least likely	Bad. Will look suspicious on resume; would need to find new employment at short notice and move to new city.
Short-term renewal	Most likely	Decent. Will provide good experience; allows for time to do a search for a long-term position elsewhere.
Long-term renewal	Somewhat likely	Excellent. Secure position in a field I enjoy; high salary; chance for promotion.

By illustrating the uncertainty surrounding her choice in this way, Lora can see that the decision is clear: accepting the short-term position is the best choice.

Sometimes decisions are highly complex. To help manage the complexity, *Smart Choices* recommends drawing a decision tree—another method of simplifying risk analysis. Consider the example of Calvin, who is planning a day of skiing for a family reunion but is concerned that there may not be enough snow. An option he is considering is an indoor ropes course. His primary objectives are to keep costs low, to find a location that is nearby (convenience), and to have fun. The uncertainty he faces is whether it will snow. If it does not snow, the family will need to travel farther to a resort that is at a higher elevation and has sufficient snow for skiing, which would increase the cost and decrease the convenience. The ropes course is close by and would be unaffected by the snow, but it is more expensive and not as much fun as the ski trip would be. Calvin has mapped out his options, the uncertainties, and the consequences in the following decision tree:[81]

---

[80] See generally SMART CHOICES, *supra* note 73 at 110.

[81] See generally SMART CHOICES, *supra* note 73 at 120.

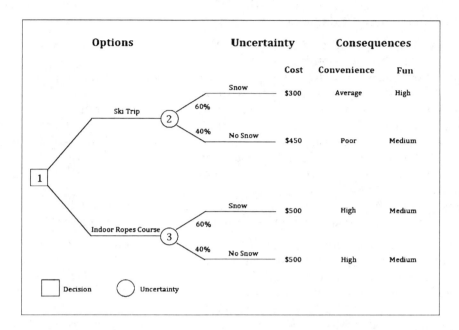

Drawing a decision tree "brings risk profiles to life."[82] Calvin can now see that the ski trip meets his objectives so much better than the ropes course that he will likely risk the 40% chance of no snow. *Smart Choices* suggests that in addition to simplifying risk analysis, the practice of sketching out a decision tree helps us think through our options in a thorough, logical way.[83]

d. Using a Fair and Effective Process

Process matters. In a negotiation or mediation, a fair and effective process can facilitate agreements on substance. Conversely, a poorly chosen process can derail talks before they even start. Lax and Sebenius discuss two types of process arrangements that represent opposing ends of a spectrum: 1) decide-announce-defend ("DAD"), and 2) full consensus ("FC").[84] With the DAD process, the negotiating parties view the matter as a private contractual arrangement between them. They don't involve other relevant stakeholders, and simply make a decision and then defend it if opposition arises. In contrast, an FC process seeks to involve all relevant stakeholders and get approval from all parties before moving forward. A

---

[82] *Id.* at 121.

[83] *Id.* at 122.

[84] 3D NEGOTIATION, *supra* note 63 at 110–112.

DAD process focuses on getting the deal done, while an FC process seeks consensus among stakeholders.[85]

Both approaches can be problematic. With the DAD process, third-party opposition can be significant enough to prevent the deal from being implemented, even if the negotiating parties reached an agreement. With an FC process, parties may not get to discuss substance because certain stakeholders are holding out. To avoid these pitfalls, there are various forms of hybrid processes along the spectrum between these two approaches. For example, rather than waiting to move forward until all stakeholders arrive at a consensus, parties could consult with other stakeholders and solicit their interests but leave the final decision making to the two parties at the table. Lax and Sebenius recommend considering the context and type of stakeholders involved to determine which type of process may be best suited for a particular deal or dispute.[86]

Sometimes process choices should be negotiated, and other times it is better to treat them in a more implicit way.[87] Lax and Sebenius suggest that it is generally better to be explicit about process choices. This helps parties feel more committed to the process and can help prevent conflicts and misunderstandings later on. However, sometimes in contentious situations, negotiating over process issues can become a major hurdle. "Process choices become proxies for other issues, and pointlessly consume valuable time."[88] They advise learning more about the party with whom you'll be negotiating to get a sense of whether they're likely to be reasonable.[89]

3D NEGOTIATION provides a process checklist that is useful in planning how a negotiation or mediation should be set up. The checklist includes the following:[90]

- **Auspices**: Where is the most appropriate forum? If the two parties are contentious, it may be best to hold the proceedings at a neutral location.
- **Mandate**: What is the intended output? Will the agreement be binding or is it meant to serve as an advisory to another party?
- **Participation**: Who will participate and in what capacity? Who will be negotiating directly? Who will be observing?
- **Decision Rules and Procedures**: How will the parties make decisions? Will they operate on an ad hoc basis, use majority vote, or use full consensus?

---

[85] *Id.* at 112.
[86] *Id.* at 112–113.
[87] *Id.* at 113.
[88] *Id.* at 113.
[89] *Id.* at 113.
[90] *Id.* at 114.

- **Agenda**: Will items to be included be negotiated? If a party wants to change the agenda, how will that be handled?
- **Staging of Process**: Should the negotiation proceed through a defined series of stages (e.g., jointly defining the problem, gathering information, negotiating agreed-upon issues, etc.), or should it proceed in an ad hoc manner?
- **External Communication**: What information can be shared outside of the negotiation? Will the sharing of information be subject to strict controls or left open to each party's discretion?
- **Process Support**: Will the parties bring in third-party support, such as a mediator, technical experts, etc.?
- **Post-deal Arrangements**: Are there implementation or adaptation issues that will occur after the agreement for which arrangements must be made?

Lax and Sebenius recommend thinking carefully about the process checklist and to determine which issues should be determined in advance, which should be negotiated, and which should be left on an ad hoc basis.[91]

EXERCISE

A "Conflict Stories" Conversation in Distributive Negotiation

This exercise illustrates what can happen in a conversation in which the parties want a fair economic resolution of a mutual problem but do not care about maintaining an ongoing relationship.

You and a partner should assume fictional names: one of you is "Smith" and the other is "Jones." Smith should read the "Confidential Information for Smith" on the following page. Jones should read the "Confidential Information for Jones" on the second page following this one.

Conduct the conversation for about five minutes. After the conversation, discuss with your partner what you experienced.

---

[91] *Id.* at 116.

"The Vicious Pit Bull" Conversation in
Distributive Negotiation

Confidential Information for Smith

Background facts for Smith:

Your neighbor Jones has a vicious pit bull dog in the front yard which is fenced but has an unlocked gate. You have complained many times to your neighbor about keeping such a dangerous dog in an unlocked yard.

You have a three-year-old child. You were home alone with your child and you took a nap on the couch. While you were asleep, your child opened the back door of your house, went next door, opened the unlocked gate, went inside the fence, and was bitten by the dog. You heard your child's screams, ran next door, and took your child to the hospital, where your child received a dozen stitches. Fortunately, there will not be any permanent, visible scarring.

Instructions for Smith:

You are furious: Jones is to blame for keeping such a dangerous dog that hurt your child. You don't care about your relationship with Jones. You are willing to settle this dispute if Jones agrees to pay you for your child's injuries and ensure this will never happen again. You are out of pocket $75.00 for the emergency room co-payment amount. You should start the negotiation by demanding that Jones pay you $1,000.00. However, if Jones is willing to put a lock on the gate, and pay you the $75.00 co-payment, you are willing to forget about what happened. Negotiate with Jones.

"The Stupid Parent" Conversation in Distributive Negotiation

Confidential Information for Jones

Background facts for Jones:

You have an American Staffordshire terrier dog in your front yard, which is fenced with a closed but unlocked gate. Your neighbor Smith has a three-year-old child who has come unattended into your yard several times to play with your dog. You have complained to Smith that the child should not be allowed to come into your yard. You also have worried about your dog biting the child, if the child played too aggressively with the dog. You could have bought a lock for the gate, but you never got around to doing that.

Smith was home alone with the child. Instead of supervising the child, Smith took a nap. While Smith slept, Smith's child got out of the house, opened your gate, went inside your fence, and was bitten by your dog. Smith woke up from the nap, ran into your yard, and took the child to the hospital for stitches on the child's face.

Instructions for Jones:

You are furious: Smith is negligent for sleeping while the child came unattended into your fenced yard through your closed gate and got hurt through no fault of yours. However, you do not want to be sued or have to make a claim against your homeowner's insurance policy, because you are afraid it might be cancelled. You also do not want Smith to complain to Animal Control about your dog. The deductible on your insurance policy is $500.00, so you would be willing to pay up to $500.00, if Smith is willing to forget about what happened. However, you should start the negotiation by saying that you are willing to put a lock on the gate so this will never happen again. Negotiate with Smith to settle this problem.

E. PUTTING IT ALL TOGETHER

EXERCISE

The following negotiation exercise requires two people, because the negotiation is between a student applicant for a clinical genetic counseling position at the UCLA Medical Genetics Clinic and the Director of the Clinic. The exercise is divided into three parts:

1.   Preparing for the negotiation.

2.   Preparing opening lines for the negotiation, giving those opening lines, and receiving feedback from the other negotiator.

3.   Conducting the negotiation and afterward discussing the experience with the other negotiator.

Preparing for the Genetic Counseling Employment Negotiation

Potential Issues to Negotiate

1.   Salary
   a.   Full-time or part-time?
   b.   Probationary period? Pay increase when you complete probationary period?
   c.   Annual pay increases?
       i.   Automatic cost-of-living increases?
       ii.   Discretionary performance ("merit") increases?
   d.   Periodic salary reviews?
   e.   Pay increase when you get your board certification?
2.   Employment Benefits
   a.   Health care?
       i.   What is covered?
       ii.   How much do you pay?
       iii.   Are your spouse (or partner) and any children covered?
   b.   Vacation days and timing?
   c.   401(k) or retirement plan?
       i.   Employer contribution?
           1.   Cash?
           2.   Stock?
       ii.   Employer match of employee's contribution?
   d.   Sick leave?
   e.   Overtime compensation, comp time off, or no compensation for overtime?
   f.   Parking?
       i.   Where?

        ii. Are parking expenses paid?
   g. Moving expenses paid? How much?
3. Professional Benefits
   a. Continuing education expenses paid?
   b. Board examination fee paid?
        i. Review course paid?
        ii. Study time off?
   c. Licensure fee paid?
   d. Malpractice insurance paid?
   e. Professional books and journals paid?
   f. Computer, cell phone, pager paid?
4. Job Responsibilities
   a. Job title?
   b. Job description?
   c. Research?
   d. Writing and publication?
   e. Travel?
   f. Hours
        i. Overtime?
        ii. Evenings?
        iii. Weekends?
        iv. On-call?
   g. Supervisor?
   h. Office location?
5. Miscellaneous Employment Issues
   a. Written confirmation of employment offer?
        i. Letter from employer confirming terms of the offer?
        ii. Email from employee confirming terms of the offer?
        iii. Deadline by which to accept the job offer?
   b. Employment "at will" or for an agreed-to period of time?
   c. Employment contract?
   d. Employee handbook?
   e. Reasons for termination?
        i. Termination for cause?
        ii. Termination without cause?
   f. Non-competition provision?
        i. Where?
        ii. How long?
   g. Non-solicitation provision?
   h. Non-disparagement provision?
   i. Employer owns intellectual property that you create?
   j. Employer's trade secrets and confidential information?
   k. Mandatory binding arbitration of employment disputes?

      1.   Prevailing-party lawyer's fees in the event of litigation or arbitration?

Confidential information for the student applicant is on the following page.

Confidential information for the Clinical Director is on the second page following this one.

Confidential Information for the Student Applicant

Scenario: *You are graduating from State University's genetic counseling program and you have been offered a clinical genetic counseling position at the LA Medical Genetics Clinic. The Genetics Clinic provides diagnostic evaluations, genetic counseling, and follow-up for individuals and families of individuals with birth defects, developmental disabilities, and inherited conditions, including ophthalmologic disorders. The Genetics Clinic currently has five MDs, two of whom also have PhD degrees. You would be the first non-doctoral professional to be hired. You are meeting with the Clinical Director, who is a physician, to negotiate the terms and conditions of your employment. The salary range in Los Angeles for a position of this kind is between $50,000 and $70,000 per year. You want to make an opening request for a salary of $70,000 per year. You are willing to accept a salary offer as low as $50,000 per year, because you do not have another job offer or even another job interview. Using the facts from your own personal identity and life situation, prepare for this negotiation as follows:*

1. Identify the issues you want to negotiate.

2. Prepare a written agenda of these negotiation issues, prioritized in terms of importance to you.

3. Review the Seven Elements and write down how you will utilize and/or apply each element.

4. Identify information you want to obtain from the Clinical Director, as well as information you do <u>not</u> want to disclose to the Clinical Director.

5. Determine whether you want to make an opening offer or whether you prefer the Clinical Director to make the opening offer. Why?

Confidential Information for the Clinical Director

Scenario: *You are meeting with a graduate student in State University's genetic counseling program to negotiate an offer of a clinical genetic counseling position at the LA Medical Genetics Clinic. The Genetics Clinic provides diagnostic evaluations, genetic counseling, and follow-up for individuals and families of individuals with birth defects, developmental disabilities, and inherited conditions, including ophthalmologic disorders. The Genetics Clinic currently has five MDs, two of whom also have PhD degrees. The Applicant would be the first non-doctoral professional to be hired by the Clinic.*

The salary range in Los Angeles for a position of this kind is between $50,000 and $70,000 per year. Given the Applicant's lack of work experience in medical genetics, you can offer up to $60,000 per year as the starting salary. You want to make an opening offer of a salary of $50,000 per year. There is a six-month probationary period during which the Applicant's employment can be terminated without cause. The Clinic pays $2,500 per year into the employee's 401(k) plan, plus full health and dental insurance benefits. The Clinic reimburses the employee's expenses for licensure, annual professional fees, and up to $1,000 for annual continuing professional education expenses. Employees get two weeks of vacation during the first three years of employment. Employees are not compensated for overtime work and do not get guaranteed comp time off for overtime. The Applicant would be expected to work one Saturday per month. You will be the Applicant's supervisor. You have three other similarly qualified applicants whom you are going to interview for this one position.

1. Review the Seven Elements and write down how you will utilize and/or apply each element.

2. Identify information you want to obtain from the Applicant.

3. Identify information you are willing to disclose to the Applicant, as well as any information you do <u>not</u> want to disclose to the Applicant.

4. Determine whether you want to make the opening offer or whether you prefer the Applicant to make one first. Why?

"Opening Lines" Exercise for the Student Applicant

Scenario: *You are graduating from State University's genetic counseling program and you are negotiating to accept a clinical genetic counseling position at the LA Medical Genetics Clinic. You are meeting with the Clinical Director to negotiate the terms and conditions of employment. Using the information identified in your preparation for this negotiation:*

1. Write your "opening lines" (i.e., the first few statements you intend to make) for this meeting:

    _____

    _____

    _____

    _____

2. Deliver your opening lines to a partner who will assume the role of the Clinical Director.

3. Your partner should jot down reactions to your opening lines and share them with you:

    _____

    _____

    _____

    _____

4. After your partner shares these reactions with you, rewrite your opening lines and deliver them again to your partner.

    _____

    _____

    _____

    _____

5. Your partner should share with you the new reactions to your rewritten opening lines.

"Opening Lines" Exercise for the Clinical Director

Scenario: *You are meeting with a graduate student in State University's genetic counseling program to negotiate the terms and conditions of employment for a clinical genetic counseling position at the LA Medical Genetics Clinic. You are the Clinical Director who is going to negotiate on behalf of the Clinic. Using the information identified in your preparation for this negotiation:*

1. Write your "opening lines" (i.e., the first few statements you intend to make) for this meeting:

   _____
   _____
   _____
   _____

2. Deliver your opening lines to a partner who will assume the role of the Applicant.

3. Your partner should jot down reactions to your opening lines and share them with you:

   _____
   _____
   _____
   _____

4. After your partner shares these reactions with you, rewrite your opening lines and deliver them again to your partner.

   _____
   _____
   _____
   _____

5. Your partner should share with you the new reactions to your rewritten opening lines.

EXERCISE

Analyzing a Mediation Training Video to Illustrate the Four Negotiation Strategies, the Seven Elements, and the Mediator's Choice of Interventions

Introduction

There are many different ways to mediate. What works for one mediator may not work for another. For example, although they have very different subject matters, many mediations start out performatively, with the parties reciting their respective conflict stories in a very confrontational, adversarial fashion. Different mediators will use different interventions to help parties improve their ability to listen and talk to one another. Some mediators will rigidly enforce procedural ground rules, such as requiring the parties to take turns talking. Other mediators may terminate the joint session and separate parties into private caucuses. Other mediators may ignore and thereby permit a lot of angry interruptions and name-calling.

Mediation also can be facilitative, analytical, evaluative, or sometimes even directive. There simply is no one-size-fits-all way of mediating. An approach that works for parties in one dispute may not work for other parties in a different dispute. For example, the mediation of a personal injury case may require a distributive negotiation strategy; mediation of a problem between two business partners may require an integrative negotiation strategy; and mediation of a relationship conflict between an employee and a supervisor may require a transformative negotiation strategy. It also helps if a mediator is competent, willing, and flexible in using different strategies and interventions in a single mediation.

Background of the Dispute

In the "Boundaries: Sexual Harassment"[92] mediation training video, the late Dr. John M. Haynes ("the mediator") intervenes using a performative negotiation strategy to help move the parties away from their conflict stories toward distributive, transformative, and integrative negotiation, which allows them ultimately to work together to repair a badly damaged academic relationship.

The parties in the mediation training video are Irene (a mature graduate student, who is a single mother) and John (one of Irene's professors in her graduate program). Irene has filed a formal sexual harassment complaint against John with the university's administration.

Irene contends that John initially invited her back to his office after class, where he closed the door, sat beside her on a "love seat," and put his hand on her knee. Later, he invited her out for coffee and then to lunch. Although she felt very uncomfortable about his frequent invitations, she did not say any-

---

[92] "Boundaries: Sexual Harassment," Positive Conflict Management, www.fongmediate. com. *See also* John M. Haynes, Gretchen L. Haynes & Larry Sun Fong, MEDIATION: POSITIVE CONFLICT MANAGEMENT 69–105 (Albany: State University of New York Press, 2004).

thing because she was afraid he would withhold his help. However, after he took her to dinner and started touching her, she decided she had to stop him from abusing his position, so she filed a sexual harassment complaint.

Although John contends that Irene has made up these "wild allegations," the university's Academic Vice President has required John to participate in mediation as a mandatory step in attempting to resolve Irene's complaint.

Comments about the Video

The mediator is a retired university professor. He has a calm, patient, and professorial demeanor in the mediation. He is willing to be assertive and even directive. Although he is not a lawyer, he knows how to leverage John's concern about the legal and reputational risks of not reaching an agreement with Irene. Without being pushed by the mediator, John would not be willing to solve the relationship problem.

A mediator's opening remarks to parties are extremely important—especially when the parties are unfamiliar with mediation—because they can clear up any misconceptions about the purpose and process of mediation. Here, the mediator's opening remarks are abbreviated, probably to fit the length of the training video. The mediator does not discuss confidentiality with the parties in his opening remarks, nor does he discuss procedural ground rules which the parties are to follow. There is no discussion of a written mediation agreement signed by the parties. Presumably these topics are not addressed due to the short length of the video.

Although he addresses Irene and John by their first names, the mediator does not instruct them to do the same. As a result, John uses Irene's first name, but Irene refers to John as "Professor Brown." For most of the video, the mediator allows John and Irene to address him and does not instruct them to talk directly to one another. However, if the parties were capable of speaking directly and effectively to one another, they might not have a relationship problem requiring mediation.

Even though this is a very emotional mediation, the mediator does not use caucuses to separate the parties. Because the parties will have an ongoing relationship as student and professor after the mediation, the mediator presumably believes the parties need to figure out how to talk to one another during the mediation so as to be able to work together afterward.

The risk from an institutional perspective of the mediator's solution to the parties' relationship problem is that John may in fact be a sexual predator who has preyed on other female students in the past and may do so again in the future. This risk is somewhat attenuated because the university knows that John has been formally accused by Irene of sexual harassment, and John knows the university will severely discipline (probably fire) him if there is another similar complaint brought against him.

The Mediator's Interventions

The mediator chooses different interventions in dealing with the two parties. The mediator permits Irene to vent a great deal, without interrupting her. The mediator also permits Irene to interrupt John frequently with emotionally charged (and often sarcastic) outbursts. The mediator tends to ignore Irene's outbursts and does not acknowledge them or restate them. This allows Irene to vent her fear, anger, and frustration directly at John, which she has never done before. She looks at John when she vents. This allows John to see and hear exactly how upset Irene is with him.

John rarely looks at Irene when he talks. He directs his remarks about Irene to the mediator almost as if she were not present. John labels and characterizes Irene's behavior, rather than describing the facts of what happened between them. The mediator interrupts John frequently. He instructs John several times, "Don't describe what you think she thinks, because that's not helpful to me."

Some student observers of the video feel the mediator is so uneven-handed in this regard that he gives the appearance he is biased toward Irene and against John. John tolerates the mediator's behavior, perhaps because John is required by the university to participate in this mandatory mediation. Other student observers feel that, by interrupting John often and by not challenging Irene's sarcastic outbursts, the mediator may be intentionally attempting to balance the power disparity between a female student and her male professor. This power balancing seems to help Irene take more responsibility for solving the relationship problem.

The mediator begins to gather information by asking broad, open-ended questions and listening to the parties' conflict stories about what happened. The parties begin the mediation with a performative orientation; each focuses on blaming the other; and each wants to "win" at the expense of the other.

Irene's conflict story is a recitation of what she characterizes as unwanted, frequent, and increasingly intimate meetings with "Professor Brown," including his touching her while sitting next to her on a small couch in his office. She intimates that John is a predator taking advantage of her by abusing the power of his position as her professor. She explains that she is afraid this situation is ruining her academic dreams and interfering with everything she has worked for as a graduate student. She implies that the only acceptable solution to the problem is to have John removed from the program.

At first, John professes ignorance about the problem and instead blames Irene. He characterizes her as paranoid and irrational. John's conflict story is that Irene is making baseless, "wild allegations" against him which are hurting his reputation in the university. By doing this, John has cast himself as the victim in his conflict story. He seems very much unaware or unwilling to accept that he has contributed anything to the relationship problem with Irene. He implies that the only acceptable solution to the problem is to have Irene removed from the program.

The mediator tells the parties they both want to reach an agreement in mediation that will enable both of them to stay in the program.

After hearing from each party, the mediator asks narrower questions to get additional factual detail and clarify the parties' respective versions of what happened. The mediator then summarizes each party's conflict story by emphasizing their important underlying interests: John is concerned about the effect of this problem on his reputation and career and he wants to continue teaching in the program he created; Irene is concerned about how she is perceived and she wants to continue as a student in the program.

After being assured by Irene that no sexual misconduct occurred, the mediator reframes the parties' conflict stories and their interests into a third story about their mutual need to work together to establish and maintain ground rules ("boundaries") for their ongoing interactions. The mediator then interprets what he has heard in a way that is acceptable to both parties, i.e., as a misunderstanding about Irene's boundaries that can be identified and respected. He does this by asking Irene a seemingly simple question, "So, you need more clear boundaries about the kinds of things to be touched and not touched?" He also volunteers that John may have "inadvertently" crossed Irene's boundaries without knowing what they were.

This neutral third story shifts the time frame from past to present, avoiding the impossible task of having to determine what actually happened and who is to blame, without diminishing the importance of Irene's emotions. The third story also reframes the parties' dispute as a problem that they are capable of resolving. Irene agrees with the mediator's reframing of the dispute, and John accepts the fact that different people have different boundaries for interpersonal interactions. The mediator's reframing of the dispute in this manner gives legitimacy to Irene's feelings, and allows John to accept this as a reasonable explanation for Irene's complaint.

Reframing the parties' dispute in this way is crucial to the success of the mediation. The initial dispute (whether or not John sexually harassed Irene) is thereby transformed from a performative conflict (about who is right and who is wrong) into a transformative conflict about the parties' relationship problem. This permits the parties to use distributive and integrative strategies about how to agree mutually on clear and comfortable ground rules in getting along together in the future. In doing so, the mediator helps the parties agree to a specific set of ground rules for their future interactions: no physical contact, no lunches or dinners, and no private meetings.

The mediator is skillful in emphasizing the reframed third story to the parties, i.e., that John inadvertently crossed Irene's undisclosed boundaries. This facilitates the parties' recognition of their proportionate contributions to their relationship problem. It also helps change their perspectives about what happened. The mediator's continual reframing and identification of the parties' mutual interests enable John and Irene to see areas of overlap and commit to begin working together in a more collaborative manner. The reframed story allows John to recognize that he inadvertently crossed Irene's boundaries which she did not disclose to him. The reframed story empowers Irene to set boundaries in her relationship with John.

The mediator does not ask the parties to engage in creative brainstorming to identify by themselves possible options that might resolve their conflict. Instead, the mediator seems persuaded there is only one feasible solution to which the parties both must commit. Irene is very unsure of herself but must learn to set limits with her professor. John must become willing and able to recognize and respect the limits set by Irene. The mediator also knows that the conflict can only be resolved if Irene becomes willing to withdraw her complaint to the university, and Irene will do that only if John commits to an agreement acceptable to her.

In a professorial, respectful, but authoritative way, the mediator educates the parties that "different people have different boundaries" and that persons in a relationship must accommodate the boundaries of the more vulnerable person. In doing this, the mediator transforms the parties' irreconcilable dispute about what happened into a shared problem about what they are willing to do in the future. The mediator then suggests and outlines the solution (i.e., setting and respecting boundaries). This allows the parties to save face and begin to work together on new ground rules for their relationship. It also avoids having to determine what actually happened in their past meetings and having to decide who is now "telling the truth."

Again and again, the mediator asks questions to elicit the parties' comments relevant to setting boundaries, restates their comments into proposed agreements about new ground rules for their future relationship, and works to get their commitment to those ground rules. By reiterating this process, the mediator helps the parties achieve greater understanding and agreement about necessary and appropriate relationship boundaries.

When John remarks that he is not sure he and Irene can ever work together again, the mediator engages in reality-testing and says, "I'm not sure you have a choice." John says that if Irene were to leave the program, the problem would go away. The mediator makes it clear to John that Irene's leaving the program is not an option. He tells John, "You're not leaving the program," and tells Irene, "You're not leaving the program." The mediator informs John that his only two choices are either to cooperate with Irene in the mediation or go to a public hearing conducted by the university. From this, John seems to understand that he really has no acceptable alternative to a negotiated agreement and that his only feasible choice is to commit to work with Irene, if he wants to avoid a public hearing. Irene's alternative to a negotiated agreement is to pursue her sexual harassment claim all the way through to litigation, which she does not prefer to do. She prefers to work with John to complete her academic program and get her degree.

The mediator asks Irene for suggestions about what she wants in her academic relationship with John. He helps Irene understand that she can and must set and articulate to John the boundaries that are comfortable for her. The mediator asks John for his cooperation as the power figure in the relationship. He helps John understand that John must respect and comply with the new boundaries set by Irene, who has less power in the relationship. John finally accepts and acknowledges that he as a professor must assume more responsibility in his relationship with his student.

In order to feel satisfied with their settlement, it is necessary for Irene to feel John has sincerely apologized and accepted responsibility for what happened. The mediator ultimately (and somewhat coercively) gets John to apologize twice to Irene for inadvertently crossing her boundaries in the past. The first time John apologizes, Irene begins to cry and explains it means a great deal to her that John is sorry for crossing her boundaries and that he did not intend her any harm. John, however, feels so uncomfortable apologizing that his apology becomes mere "regret" and he again brings up again Irene's "wild allegations." Because John's first apology seems insincere and incomplete, the mediator pushes John to make a second apology. The mediator explains to John that he needs to recognize that Irene's feelings are legitimate. John replies that had he known she was uncomfortable, he would never have done what he did and he never meant to upset her. John's second, seemingly sincere expression of regret is sufficient for Irene.

The "boundaries" solution—which the mediator suggested and the parties accepted—restores to Irene her comfort in being a student and receiving John's academic help. Although the parties do not enter into a formal written agreement as part of the mediation training video, the transformation of their academic relationship should ensure they will be able to work together productively as professor and student, with little likelihood that their relationship problem will be repeated.

The Mediator's Use of the Seven Elements of Negotiation

Transforming the Parties' Relationship

Relationship is one of the Harvard Negotiation Project's Seven Elements of negotiation. The mediator quickly identifies the parties' conflicted past relationship and their need to transform it into a viable academic relationship going forward. The mediator recognizes that the parties' past relationship is the real basis of their dispute—Irene and John have different expectations about their relationship that have created misunderstandings and conflict.

The relationship between John and Irene during the mediation is very emotional in different ways. John is defensive and accusatory. John voices his emotions when he says he is very worried about Irene's allegations and their effect on his reputation. Irene feels both angry and disrespected. She uses the word "feel" many times in explaining her point of view. Generally, the mediator allows both parties to vent their feelings and does not intervene when emotions run high. Although the parties' emotions are not the focal point of their dispute, the mediator recognizes that Irene's feelings (i.e., that John does not respect her autonomy and he refuses to accept any accountability) must be addressed as part of an agreement in mediation.

Improving the Parties' Communication

The parties' performative communication (i.e., telling and retelling their respective conflict stories) prevents them from listening, seeing the other's perspective, and engaging in problem-solving. Their performative communication is not only verbal but nonverbal as well, e.g., John rarely looks at Irene and instead seems to ignore the fact that she is sitting next to him. The mediator tolerates Irene's frequent emotional interruptions when John says something with which she disagrees. Some observers of the video feel this shows the mediator is biased toward Irene and against John. Other observers feel this shows the mediator is balancing the power disparity between Irene and John, which empowers Irene to take more responsibility for solving the relationship problem.

The mediator confronts John several times with his need to recognize that Irene has the right to set the boundaries in their relationship and that John inadvertently crossed Irene's undisclosed boundaries, for which he should apologize to Irene for the misunderstanding and discomfort he unintentionally caused. When John's first apology does not seem sincere and well-meaning, the mediator instructs John to apologize a second time in a more meaningful way.

The mediator is very effective in actively listening to both John and Irene, asking probing questions, summarizing what he has heard, clarifying what the parties want, and identifying their underlying interests.

Identifying the Parties' Interests

The mediator effectively identifies and explores Irene's concerns, objectives, needs, desires, and fears, but does not do the same with John. The mediator does not explore John's expressed fears and concerns, but instead leverages John's concern that the university administration will proceed with a public hearing against him if he does not agree to resolve Irene's complaint to her satisfaction. It is not until late in the mediation that John expresses his desire to put this problem to rest once and for all.

The mediator helps Irene climb down the ladder of accusation to disclose and discuss her underlying interests in staying in the graduate program and having an academic relationship with John as her professor. Because Irene frequently accuses John of being selfish and setting all of the rules, the mediator treats her complaint as a request to set the rules in the parties' relationship. The mediator then encourages and assists Irene in setting those boundaries. The mediator also identifies that, in addition to setting clear boundaries in their relationship going forward, Irene needs to hear John acknowledge that her feelings are legitimate and that he must sincerely apologize for the discomfort he has unintentionally caused her.

Using John's Unacceptable Alternative

John's best alternative to a negotiated agreement (BATNA) is to proceed to a public hearing by the university on Irene's sexual harassment complaint, which is unacceptable to John. When John seems unwilling to engage in problem-solving with Irene, the mediator twice raises John's unacceptable BATNA to leverage John's willingness to accept the boundaries set by Irene for their academic relationship going forward.

Irene's BATNA (which is the same as John's) is to proceed to a public hearing on her complaint. She is willing to do this, although she strongly prefers negotiating a new academic relationship with John.

Using Legitimacy Information

The mediator, who is a retired university professor, reminds John several times that different students have different boundaries about what is acceptable conduct in an academic relationship with a professor. The mediator also reminds John that a student has the right to set the boundaries in such a relationship, and that the professor (who is in a position of power) is obligated to respect the student's boundaries. By providing this legitimacy information in the manner he does, the mediator is being evaluative (i.e., he is critiquing John's behavior with Irene) and even directive (i.e., he basically is advising John to change his behavior with Irene).

Generating Options

The mediator helps Irene generate options for an acceptable academic relationship with John: no lunches, no dinners, no physical contact, and no socializing. When John objects to Irene's request that they meet in his office only during daytime hours, Irene generates a responsive option that she will meet with John and another mature student in his office after normal hours.

Because the mediator understands that Irene also needs to hear John accept responsibility for causing her discomfort, the mediator generates an apology option by asking John whether it would be appropriate for him to apologize directly to Irene for inadvertently crossing her boundaries in their academic relationship. After John makes an insincere apology, John revises the apology option and expresses his sincere regret for having inadvertently crossed Irene's undisclosed boundaries.

Leveraging John's Commitment

John does not commit to accept Irene's terms for an acceptable academic relationship until the mediator underscores the fact that John has an unacceptable BATNA (i.e., proceeding to a public hearing) and provides John with legitimacy information (i.e., that a student has the right set the boundaries in an academic relationship with a professor).

Use of the Four Strategies of Negotiation

Performative Negotiation

Irene's and John's narrations of their respective conflict stories are classic performative negotiation. The conflict stories express their separate perceptions of reality. The stories do not try to be factually fair, accurate, or complete. Both parties cast themselves as the victim in their relationship.

John denies any wrongdoing, and Irene justifies her acquiescence to John's social invitations in terms of her fear that he would withdraw his academic help if she objected. They each conceal their contribution to their relationship conflict, and neither takes any responsibility for problem-solving. They focus on the past and who is to blame. The mediator intervenes into their performative negotiation by using effective active listening and by encouraging them to engage in problem-solving by asking questions and making comments based on their respective interests and concerns. Throughout the mediation, the parties return to their performative style of communication, and the mediator intervenes again and again to get them back to problem-solving negotiation.

Distributive Negotiation

The mediator uses distributive negotiation strategy when he engages Irene in identifying specific boundaries that she wants in an acceptable academic relationship with John. The mediator also uses distributive negotiation strategy when he leverages John's commitment to accept Irene's boundaries by reminding John that his BATNA is unacceptable.

Integrative Negotiation

Irene uses integrative negotiation strategy by generating a responsive option that she will meet with John and another mature student in his office after normal hours. The mediator uses integrative negotiation strategy in getting John to apologize directly to Irene for inadvertently crossing her boundaries. John uses integrative negotiation strategy when he revises the apology option and expresses his regret for having inadvertently crossed Irene's boundaries.

Transformative Negotiation

After John accepts Irene's boundaries for an academic relationship going forward, and after John expresses regret for the discomfort he inadvertently caused Irene, the parties agree that they have transformed and reconstructed their academic relationship into one that is feasible and probably self-enforcing. John remarks that Irene is a good student and a nice person about whom he has always thought highly. He acknowledges that her past concerns now seem genuine to him. He seems to understand that, despite his good intentions, the impact of his prior behavior was hurtful to Irene. Irene agrees that she will tell John if there is anything in their future relationship that troubles her. John agrees he does not want to do anything that inadvertently troubles Irene.

Conclusion

The mediator in this training video moves fluidly back and forth between mediation strategies and techniques, knowing when to listen, when to ask questions, when to make comments, and when and how to push John to commitment. The mediator spends the first half of the mediation understanding each party's perspective so he can identify their five major areas of concern: no more touching; no more invitations to lunches and dinners; no more wild allegations; future feasible academic consultations; and confidentiality. The mediator invents a third story (i.e., setting and respecting relationship boundaries) that is sufficiently neutral and comprehensive that it engages both parties' issues and interests and allows each party to save face. He poses possible solutions as questions (e.g., in asking Irene whether she wants clearer boundaries, and in asking John whether he is willing to apologize to Irene). The mediator tolerates a great deal of emotional venting without going into caucus, and he simply ignores the parties' emotional cross-accusations (e.g., John accuses Irene of paranoia, and Irene accuses John of lying).

The mediation is an instructive illustration of how the Seven Elements, the four strategies, and various negotiation and mediation skills can be used effectively in resolving a high-conflict dispute.

CHAPTER 4

DEALING WITH DIFFICULT TACTICS[1]

■ ■ ■

Boxer Mike Tyson once famously remarked, "Everyone has a plan until they get punched in the face." Despite careful planning and preparation, sometimes you may encounter parties whose negotiation style or tactics catch you off guard. Some people with whom you negotiate will be "difficult negotiators" because:

- they are inexperienced or unprepared and, therefore, are naively unrealistic;
- they are overly aggressive positional bargainers who refuse to budge from intentionally unrealistic initial demands;
- they are extremely competitive and believe that negotiation is a win-lose game that they "win" only if you "lose;"
- they choose to use manipulation or deception to attempt to take advantage of you;
- they do not have legitimacy information about fair market value or precedents, so they make uninformed, unrealistic demands; or
- they overestimate the strength of their alternative or underestimate the strength of yours, so they incorrectly believe they have more leverage over you than they actually have.

Fortunately, there are strategies, conceptual tools, and specific skills you can use when dealing with difficult negotiators. This section discusses several effective approaches.

1. BECOME FAMILIAR WITH DIFFICULT TACTICS

An important first step toward defusing difficult tactics is becoming aware of the various approaches commonly used by parties who are difficult negotiators. Because difficult tactics tend to throw us off balance and can be confusing or disorienting, simply identifying and putting a name to the dynamic can help restore a sense of order within ourselves, and provides some clarity about next steps and how to respond. Goodpaster explains the importance of familiarizing oneself with hard bargaining tactics:

---

[1] See generally William Ury, GETTING PAST NO: NEGOTIATING WITH DIFFICULT PEOPLE (New York: Bantam Books, 1991), and from Arthur L. Costa and Bena Kallick, HABITS OF MIND, http://www.habitsofmind.org/resources/OTHER/16HOM2.pdf (last visited March 6, 2013).

Recognizing the moves the other party is using helps you figure out their game and game plan. You can then play that game, if you choose, or at least protect yourself and defend your interests. If you think you can better achieve your aims by negotiating in a different way, you can seek to change the negotiation game.[2]

Although there is a wide range of tough tactics that a party might employ,[3] Ury suggests that all tactics can be classified into three basic categories:[4]

1. **Stone Walls:** stubborn refusal to move from a stated position
   - "It's company policy."
   - "Take it or leave it."
   - "We'll get back to you."

2. **Attacks:** pressuring a party in order to intimidate, confuse, or make her uncomfortable
   - Threats ("Do it or else. . . ")
   - Credibility or status ("You haven't been in this job long, have you?")

3. **Tricks:** attempts to deceive or take advantage of a party
   - Manipulating data
   - No authority (party gets as much information from you as possible, then claims he doesn't have authority to come to a final agreement and needs to consult with his supervisor; an attempt to "get another bite at the apple")
   - Last-minute add-ons (party tries to extract additional concessions to a deal when she led you to believe it was already final)

Once we identify and categorize the tactic, we can proceed to think through the most appropriate way to respond. As mentioned previously, the simple act of recognizing and naming the tactic can be a substantial step toward defusing it; however, usually more work is needed to respond effectively. The following sections discuss additional tools that can be useful in dealing with difficult tactics.

---

[2]   Gary Goodpaster, *A Primer on Competitive Bargaining*, 1996 J. DISP. RESOL. 325, 350.

[3]   Goodpaster identifies a long list of various tactics and provides a brief explanation of each. For example, his list includes precondition demands; you first; first offer—large demand; anchoring; false demand, false concession; late hit; low-balling; linkage; salami; Boulwarism; split the difference; false scarcity; final offer; misleading concession pattern; red herring; and many others. The list provides an instructive look at the range of tactics one might encounter when dealing with a difficult negotiator. *Id.* at 349–369

[4]   Ury, *supra* note 1 at 40–41.

2. GO TO THE BALCONY TO SEE WHAT SHOULD BE CHANGED AT THE NEGOTIATION TABLE

The "Go to the Balcony" chapter of *Getting Past No*[5] deals with the interactions of reciprocity, awareness, and choices about negotiation strategy and tactics.

When a difficult negotiator attacks you, your instinctive reaction is to attack back. This is called negative-reactive reciprocity. This kind of negative response usually makes matters worse and often leads to a futile confrontation with the other negotiator. This does not advance your self-interest and impairs the hope of having a productive negotiating relationship. Negative-reactive reciprocity also can make you "stupid" in the midst of conflict, because you lose or diminish your objectivity when you become angry or upset.

So, when you find yourself dealing with a difficult negotiator, you can step back, collect your thoughts, get your emotions in check, and look at the situation objectively. William Ury analogizes this to climbing onto a balcony and looking down at the negotiation table from above. From the perspective of the "balcony," you can be detached momentarily from the conflict and calmly evaluate what is happening. This kind of awareness enables you to see yourself, the other negotiator, and your interactions. You then can think constructively about how to change the interactions in order to fix the problems in the negotiation.

From the balcony overlooking the negotiation table, you can decide to:

- pause and say nothing;
- mentally review the negotiation up to this point to identify the problems;
- take a break or take a walk and calm down;
- reschedule the negotiation to another day; or
- talk with the difficult negotiator about the problems you observe and ask his advice about how best to proceed.

From the balcony, as though you were a mediator coaching yourself in the negotiation, you can use the Seven Elements of negotiation to diagnose what is causing the problems at the negotiation table. For example, do the problems deal with:

- **Relationship:** Are the parties not being respectful to one another?
- **Communication:** Are the parties not taking turns listening and talking?
- **Interests:** Have the parties not identified and discussed what they want?

---

[5] *Id.* at 31.

- **Options:** Have the parties not identified productive ways of working together?
- **Legitimacy:** Do the parties lack objective information about market value or precedents?
- **Alternatives:** Have the parties overestimated the strengths of their BATNAs?
- **Commitment:** Are the parties unwilling to negotiate productively at this time?

The authors of *Habits of Mind* describe three sets of characteristics, skills, and behaviors that are useful when you decide to go to the balcony. These include:

- **Managing Impulsivity:** Effective negotiators are deliberate. They are calm and thoughtful. They think before they act. They have a vision of the outcome, goal, or destination they want to achieve, before they react. They consider their interests, alternatives, and the consequences of various choices, before taking action. They then develop a plan.
- **Thinking about Thinking:** Effective negotiators think about what they want to accomplish. They make real-time comparative judgments about what they are doing and how they can do it more productively. They monitor the effects of their behavior on others. They reflect on how to improve their performance. They can change course when their negotiation strategy is not working as planned.
- **Persisting:** Effective negotiators stick to the task until it is completed. They analyze the problems in the negotiation and develop a plan to fix them. If their initial approach to the negotiation does not work, they try another. They collect more information and look for new approaches. They don't give up. They keep trying.

3. SEE WHAT THE NEGOTIATION LOOKS LIKE FROM THE PERSPECTIVE OF THE OTHER SIDE OF THE TABLE

Another way to deal with a difficult negotiator is to try to see things from his perspective. The "Step to Their Side" chapter in *Getting Past No*[6] deals with active listening and with understanding and acknowledging the other negotiator's point of view.

If a difficult negotiator feels that you understand and acknowledge his point of view (even though you do not agree with it), he may be less reactive, more rational, and more responsive to problem-solving. Once he feels that you have understood and acknowledged his perspective, he is

---

[6]   Ury, *supra* note 1 at 52.

more likely to be willing to listen to you. When expressing your views and referring to his views, you can replace "but" with "and" so that what he hears is not criticism or disagreement, but rather your expression of your point of view together with his. When you speak about yourself, speak from the first-person position and say things like, "I feel that . . . " This is less threatening than when you speak from the second-person position and say things like, "You did . . . " You are less likely to provoke a negative response when speaking from the first-person position. Also, speaking about what happened in the past, or who is to blame, is generally counterproductive, so speak about the present (e.g., about what you want) and the future (e.g., about what you are willing to do).

The authors of *Habits of Mind* describe three more sets of characteristics, skills, and behaviors that are useful in perspective-taking and effective communication:

- **Listening with Empathy and Understanding:** Effective negotiators listen to and understand others. They try to see the other's point of view. They acknowledge the other's thoughts and emotions. They listen to the "music" of emotions that plays underneath the other person's words. They look for clues. They are willing to consider the merits of another's ideas and build upon them.

- **Thinking Flexibly:** Effective negotiators perceive the world from multiple perspectives. They can take a bird's-eye view of themselves and their interactions with others. They can change their mind as they consider new information. They value intuition and hunches. They have a high tolerance of confusion and ambiguity.

- **Questioning and Probing:** Effective negotiators seek accurate information underlying their own and others' assumptions and conclusions. They ask questions from various perspectives, inquire about causes and effects, and consider hypothetical consequences (i.e., "what ifs"). They recognize when they don't know or don't understand something, and they seek additional relevant information.

The ladder of inference (discussed in Chapter Three) also can be a powerful and effective tool in viewing the situation from the other side's perspective, and asking questions that help you and the other party "climb down the ladder" to see how you might have arrived at different conclusions.

4. NAME THE GAME

One way to defuse a difficult tactic is to "name the game."[7] By explicitly identifying to the other party what you think is happening, you can

---

[7]　*Id.* at 39.

encourage the difficult negotiator to take a more productive approach. It is generally more effective to avoid being accusatory; rather, simply describe how the dynamic feels to you, and then suggest a better way to proceed. For example, if it seems as though the other side is using a "good cop / bad cop" routine, you could say to them, "It feels like you are deliberately taking an extreme position so that your partner comes across as reasonable. We could adopt the same approach, too, but it seems like both sides would end up wasting a lot of time playing that game. It might be more productive if we communicate in a straightforward way so that we can get a better sense of each other's real interests and start generating options that will work for both of us."

5.   DON'T REJECT THE DIFFICULT NEGOTIATOR'S DEMANDS; REFRAME THEM AS REQUESTS

Another tool you can use in dealing with a difficult negotiator is called "reframing," The "Don't Reject: Reframe" chapter of *Getting Past No* deals with reframing a difficult negotiator's statement of positions or demands to create possible options that might satisfy both negotiators' important interests. Reframing means recasting what the other person says into a form that directs attention back to the mutual problem of satisfying both parties' interests.

Negotiators sometimes frame their position as a demand or accusation that blames the other person, e.g., "*You forced me to quit because of a hostile workplace.*" Not surprisingly, the listener responds with a denial and a counter-demand or accusation, e.g., "*That's not true. You are lazy and incompetent and you couldn't do the work. That's why you quit.*"

By contrast, reframing strips out the speaker's negative emotion and accusatory language and expresses the speaker's unstated underlying interests. A helpful step in reframing is asking a problem-solving question that focuses attention on the interests of each side and the options for satisfying those interests. The listener could reframe the first speaker's accusation into a statement that expresses both parties' concerns and interests, e.g., "*We both are upset that the employment situation did not work out. What can we do about it now?*"

Reframing focuses on the parties' problem, not on the character of the people involved. It engages the first speaker's willingness to look at the problem from a new perspective. It enables the listener to hear and acknowledge the speaker's concerns. It opens up an opportunity for dialogue about the parties' unexpressed needs, desires, or fears, thereby increasing the likelihood of mutual problem-solving. Some suggestions for reframing demands or accusations into requests are discussed in Chapter Three.

A *Habits of Mind* concept that is useful in reframing is "Thinking and Speaking with Clarity and Precision."[8] Effective negotiators know that language and thinking are intertwined. They know that language specificity and word-choice control enhance negotiation. They strive for clear, accurate communication. They avoid vague and imprecise language, generalizations, distortions, and exaggerations. They are disciplined about word choices because they know the differing impacts, for example, of saying "That's a novel idea" versus saying "That's a naïve idea."

6.　DEVISE A SOLUTION THAT SATISFIES THE DIFFICULT NEGOTIATOR'S IMPORTANT INTERESTS

Focusing on the other party's interests and finding ways to make it easier for him to come to an agreement is another way to deal with difficult tactics. The "Build Them a Golden Bridge" chapter of *Getting Past No*[9] deals with devising an agreement that becomes the opponent's idea, satisfies his most important interests, and helps him save face. Suggestions for doing this include:

- Assume the difficult negotiator wants an acceptable agreement and also wants to feel he was treated fairly in the negotiation.
- Elicit the difficult negotiator's ideas and interests and begin to build on them. Start with his ideas that you find most constructive and begin devising options that achieve an outcome that satisfies his interests and is fair to you.
- Look for low-cost/high-benefit ways to expand the pie. Identify things you can give the difficult negotiator that are of significant benefit to him but have a low cost to you. In return, obtain things that are of significant benefit to you but are of low cost to him.
- You can allow a difficult negotiator to save face by pretending not to notice his difficult behaviors.

A *Habits of Mind* concept that can be helpful in devising an outcome which satisfies both parties' important interests is "Creating, Imagining and Innovating."[10] Effective negotiators develop and use their capacity to create original, ingenious solutions. They can start with a vision of a desired outcome and create a path to get there by working backward. In brainstorming, they are willing to try novel approaches to solving problems.

8　Costa and Kallick, *supra* note 1.

9　Ury, supra note 1 at 105.

10　Costa and Kallick, *supra* note 1.

7. PROVIDE PRINCIPLED REASONS TO MOTIVATE A DIFFICULT NEGOTIATOR TO REACH AN AGREEMENT

Finally, helping a difficult negotiator see the likely outcome, if an agreement is not reached, can be an effective way to deal with his hardball tactics. The "Use Power to Educate" chapter in *Getting Past No*[11] deals with helping a difficult negotiator to find additional motivation to reach an agreement by avoiding the negative consequences of having no agreement at all.

Sometimes the difficult negotiator does not have sufficient factual information about the problem to enable him to see all the risks of not reaching an agreement, so respectfully disclose this information to educate him. Assume the difficult negotiator has miscalculated how best to achieve his own interests, so focus his attention on avoiding the negative consequences of not having an agreement. One way to do this is by asking questions designed to get him to think through the adverse impact of the negative consequences on him.

Sometimes a difficult negotiator does not have legitimacy information about what is an objectively fair agreement for both parties. Or he may assume that you do not have such legitimacy information and, therefore, he assumes he can take advantage of you by being extremely aggressive in his negotiating position. In either case, share legitimacy information and discuss your willingness to reach an agreement that conforms to objective standards of fairness (e.g., published fair-market values).

Sometimes a difficult negotiator has overestimated the strength of his BATNA (or is bluffing about what he says is the strength of his alternative). Ask him to explain his alternative in detail and then carefully evaluate whether you have overlooked something relevant that could change your views. If he has overestimated the strength of his BATNA, you can show him how reaching an agreement is better for achieving his interests than electing his weaker BATNA.

Sometimes a difficult negotiator has underestimated the strength of your BATNA. Ask him what he thinks you will do if you do not reach an agreement. Then make a clear, direct statement of what you intend to do if there is no agreement. You can explain why you prefer your BATNA over the offer he is demanding that you accept. This should be done respectfully and thoughtfully, because he will perceive this information as a threat (i.e., you indirectly are threatening to end the negotiation unless he makes more movement toward a mutually acceptable agreement).

The authors of *Habits of Mind* describe two sets of characteristics, skills, and behaviors that are useful in using information that may be perceived to be negative to motivate additional movement toward an agreement:

---

[11]   *Id.* at 130.

- **Applying Past Knowledge:** Effective negotiators use what they know and learn from experience. They make choices and explanations based on prior knowledge. They can abstract meaning from experience and apply it to a novel situation.

- **Taking Responsible Risks:** Effective negotiators go beyond the limits of the status quo. They constantly expand their competence. They are willing to take risks by trying new things. They venture into situations where they can fail. They view setbacks as interesting and educational experiences from which they can grow.

Difficult negotiators can be difficult in a wide range of ways. By learning the various tactics that difficult negotiators often employ, we can better prepare ourselves to respond effectively with some of the tools and approaches discussed here. While there is no single blueprint for managing a difficult negotiator, diversifying our toolbox can better enable us to negotiate with confidence, regardless of the approach taken by the party on the other side of the table.

EXERCISE

The Lion Tamer

This exercise requires three participants who will each play one of three roles: a lion, a lion tamer, and a coach. Each person should identify a conflict scenario in which she has been involved where the opposing party was especially difficult (e.g., a landlord-tenant dispute where the landlord was the opposing party and used a take-it-or-leave-it approach, or a dispute with a customer service representative who adamantly insists he cannot do anything to fix your problem because of "company policy," etc.). Each group should designate one person as the lion, one as the lion tamer, and one as the coach. The lion should explain her conflict scenario to the others, and then the lion and the lion tamer will do a five-minute negotiation role-play with the lion as the difficult party and the lion tamer using problem-solving tactics discussed in this book to attempt to resolve the dispute. The coach should take notes during the role-play and then provide feedback to the parties in a debriefing discussion immediately following the role-play. After debriefing, each person should switch roles (e.g., the lion tamer becomes the coach, the coach becomes the lion, and the lion becomes the lion tamer), and then proceed with another round as instructed above.

EXERCISE

Responding to Manipulation and Deception[12]

Manipulation and Deception Examples	Your response?
1. **Preconditions**—"I will negotiate if you first agree to do . . ."	
2. **Boulwarism**—"This is the only offer I'm going to make; you must agree to it now, or I'm walking out."	
3. **Matter of Principle**—"My client doesn't care how much it will cost; this is a matter of principle to her."	
4. **Better Facts**—"I have better information about this than you do . . . "	
5. **New Evidence**—"Let me show you a document you haven't seen before."	
6. **Greater Credibility**—"Who is more likely to be believed by a jury, your client or mine?"	
7. **The Right Rule**—"You are applying the wrong rule in making your evaluation. I'll apply the right one."	
8. **Insider Knowledge**—"This is not how the system works here. I'll explain it to you."	
9. **Bad Publicity/Ruined Reputation**—"Your client's reputation will be ruined if this goes to trial."	
10. **Delay**—"If you don't agree to settle, this will drag out in the courts for years."	
11. **Direct Costs**—"The cost of lawyers and experts in this case will be astronomical; you can't afford that."	

---

[12] See generally John Wade, "Mapping the Deceptive Dance of Hard Bargainers," 19 BOND DISPUTE RESOLUTION NEWS (May 2005) (http://www.bond.edu.au/law/centres/drc/newsletter/Vol19May05.pdf).

Manipulation and Deception Examples	Your response?
12. **Indirect Costs**—"To litigate this will take your client away from her business for weeks; she can't do that."	
13. **Hassle/Stress Aversion**—"You're going to have to live with this ongoing mess unless it's settled now."	
14. **Third–Party Effects**—"What will your customers do when they are subpoenaed for depositions?"	
15. **Nothing to Lose**—"If you win, I'll just file for bankruptcy and you'll get nothing."	
16. **Indifference**—"Your client needs to settle; my client doesn't care if we settle this or not."	
17. **More Resources**—"My client has the money and will spend whatever it takes to win this case."	
18. **Better Law**—"If this goes to trial, I'm going to win because the law is on my side."	
19. **Risk and Loss Survivability**—"My client can survive a bad outcome if this goes to court, but yours can't."	
20. **Precedent Floodgate**—"I can't create a bad precedent by agreeing to do that."	
21. **Outside Control or Influence**—"I'd like to, but my boss would fire me if . . . "	
22. **Stronger Alternative**—"I can do better than that elsewhere . . . "	
23. **Good Cop/Bad Cop**—"If you don't work with me, you're going to have to deal with . . . "	
24. **Threats/Bluffs**—If you don't settle right now, I'm going to sue you for everything you've got."	
25. **Expertise**—"We've hired the best expert in the	

Manipulation and Deception Examples	Your response?
country to testify . . . "	
26. **Loss of Client Control**—"If we don't reach an agreement now, I can't control what my client will do."	
27. **Escalation Commitment**—"If you don't settle this today, my client told me to file a complaint tomorrow."	
28. **Jury Irrationality**—"Juries are so unpredictable in cases like this; things could go really badly for you."	
29. **Final Concession**—"If your client will agree to do one more thing, we have a deal."	
30. **Other examples** you've experienced—	

CHAPTER 5

USING PRINCIPLES OF RECIPROCITY IN NEGOTIATION AND MEDIATION

■ ■ ■

1. WHAT IS RECIPROCITY?

Reciprocity affects both the process of negotiation (and mediation) and its substantive outcome. Reciprocity fuels negotiation (for good or bad) because it affects the nature of the relationship between negotiators, the quality of their communication, their willingness to share information and engage in problem-solving, and their commitment to the negotiating process.

Reciprocity is "the almost universal belief that people should be paid back for what they do, that one good (or bad) deed deserves another. This belief is held by people in primitive and not-so-primitive societies all around the world, and it serves as the grease that allows [negotiation and mediation] wheels to turn smoothly. Because people expect that their actions will be paid back in one form or another, influence is possible."[1]

Reciprocity can be positive, i.e., proactively doing a good deed first or reactively paying back one good deed with another. It also can be negative, i.e., proactively acting badly first or proactively paying back one bad deed with another. These four variables generate four kinds of reciprocity:

- Positive proactive reciprocity ("Do unto others as you would have them do unto you.")
- Positive reactive reciprocity ("Always return a favor.")
- Negative proactive reciprocity ("Shoot first; ask questions later.")
- Negative reactive reciprocity ("An eye for an eye; a tooth for a tooth.")

2. THE UNIVERSALITY OF RECIPROCITY

Reciprocity appears to be part of human nature, perhaps instinctive or primal. For example, there is near-unanimity among the world's religions about how one person should treat another. Most world religions have scriptural passages in their holy texts, or sayings of their leaders, which

---

[1] Allan R. Cohen & David L. Bradford, *Influence without Authority: The Use of Alliances, Reciprocity, and Exchange to Accomplish Work*, reprinted in NEGOTIATION READINGS, EXERCISES AND CASES (2nd ed.) edited by Roy J. Lewicki, et al. (Illinois: Irwin, Inc., 1993) at 355.

promote the principle of positive proactive reciprocity, which is often called "the Golden Rule:"

- **Adventists**—When Adventists become leaders or exert influence in their wider society, this should be done in a manner consistent with the golden rule. Declaration of the Seventh-day Adventist Church on Church–State Relations.

- **Baha'i**—Lay not on any soul a load that you would not wish to be laid upon you, and desire not for anyone the things you would not desire for yourself. *Baha'u'llah*, Gleanings.

- **Buddhism**—Treat not others in ways that you yourself would find hurtful. *Udana–Varga*, 5,1.

- **Christianity**—In everything, do to others as you would have them do to you; for this is the law and the prophets. *Matthew*, 7:12.

- **Confucianism**—One word which sums up the basis of all good conduct . . . *loving kindness*. Do not do to others what you do not want done to yourself. *Analects*, 15.23.

- **Hinduism**—This is the sum of duty: do not do to others what would cause pain if done to you. *Mahabharata*, 5:1517.

- **Islam**—Not one of you truly believes until you wish for others what you wish for yourself. *Hadith*.

- **Jainism**—One should treat all creatures in the world as one would like to be treated. *Sutrakritanga*.

- **Judaism**—What is hateful to you, do not do to your neighbor. This is the entire Law; all the rest is commentary. *Talmud, Shabbat* 3id.

- **Latter-day Saints**—Therefore, all things whatsoever ye would that men should do to you, do ye even so to them, for this is the law and the prophets. 3 *Nephi* 14:12.

- **Taoism**—Regard your neighbor's gain as your own gain, and your neighbor's loss as your own loss. *T'aiShang Kan Ying P'ien*, 213–218.

- **Zoroastrianism**—Do not do unto others whatever is injurious to yourself. *Dadisten–I–dinik*, 94,5.

3. SOURCES AND EXPLANATIONS OF RECIPROCITY

As infants we learn socialized patterns of positive proactive and reactive reciprocity in our relationships with our mothers and others who smile at us:

> When your baby's about two months old, he may begin to converse with you in a language that's part gesture and part wordless sounds. He knows that smiling makes you react, so he smiles at you a lot.

Then you smile back. He smiles again . . . Babies at this age are delighted to be around people, be they parents or strangers. They're likely to smile at anyone who smiles at them.[2]

These patterns can persist in adulthood. As adults we continually are amazed at how many strangers we walk past on the sidewalk who return our smiles in a seemingly warm and genuine manner.

We also may be physiologically "hard-wired" to cooperate with one another. Scientists have studied the neural activity of subjects who were playing the classic negotiation game called "Prisoner's Dilemma." In the game, which is a simple and elegant model of reciprocity, participants can select competitive or cooperative strategies to pursue personal financial gain. In their brain-imaging studies, researchers found that when test subjects engaged in a cooperative strategy, two broad areas of the brain were activated. Both areas are rich in neurons able to respond to dopamine, the brain chemical involved in addictive behaviors. When asked afterward how they felt while playing the game, the subjects often described feeling good when they cooperated. In other words, the study suggests that people cooperate because it feels good to do so.[3]

Economists have attempted to explain the readily observable behavior that people often cooperate rather than always compete. The Oxford economist Francis Ysidro Edgeworth first posed the problem of the "bargain" in 1881. Edgeworth understood that—growing out of their separate individual self-interests—people collaborate, cooperate, and make deals. The parties to a bargain act on the expectation that their cooperation will yield more than by their acting alone.[4] Similarly, in 1949, John Forbes Nash, Jr., explained in his paper called "The Bargaining Problem"[5] that two individuals can collaborate for mutual benefit in more than one way. How they split the gain in a bargaining situation reflects how much the deal is worth to each individual, which in turn depends on a combination of the negotiators' back-up alternatives and the potential benefits of striking a deal.[6] Nash (who is the subject of the film, "A Beautiful Mind") received the Nobel Prize for his equilibrium theorem about games that involve a mix of cooperation and competition.

The principle of reciprocity also underlies the "tit-for-tat" dynamics of game theory. *Either* I choose to act toward the other party first in the

---

[2] *See e.g.* THE CHILDREN'S HOSPITAL GUIDE TO YOUR CHILD'S HEALTH AND DEVELOPMENT 99, 102 (Alan D. Woolf, Howard C. Shane, Margaret A. Kenna and Kathleen Cahill Allison eds.) (Boston: Children's Hospital, 2010).

[3] Natalie Angier, *Why We're So Nice: We're Wired to Cooperate*, THE NEW YORK TIMES (July 23, 2002).

[4] Sylvia Nasar, A BEAUTIFUL MIND: THE LIFE OF MATHEMATICAL GENIUS AND NOBEL LAUREATE JOHN NASH 89 (New York: Touchstone, 1998).

[5] John Forbes Nash, Jr., *The Bargaining Problem*, 18 ECONOMETRICA 155–62 (1950).

[6] A BEAUTIFUL MIND, *SUPRA* NOTE 4 AT 99.

manner in which I would like them to react to me, *or* I tend to react in kind to how the other person initially treats me. Tit-for-tat positive proactive reciprocity is a kind of "modeling" of preferred behavior, a "teaching" strategy, a form of "coaching," or a kind of "self-fulfilling prophecy" in which I attempt to influence others to act the way I treat them, in the manner I wish them to react. Tit-for-tat negative reactive reciprocity is a kind of "sanctioning" of unacceptable behavior in which I attempt to influence others to change the way they treat me, by showing them the adverse consequences of their negative behavior, i.e., their negative behavior creates "costs" to them they may prefer to avoid.

Anthropologist Polly Wiessner has written about reciprocity in human culture.[7] She notes sociologist Marcel Mauss' formula for reciprocity presented in his 1925 work entitled "The Gift," in which he argued that humans have a threefold need to give, receive, and reciprocate in order to form social relationships. In these relationships, people give in order to make friends, and people make friends in order to get gifts and assistance. Wiessner describes how these reciprocal relationships among the !Kung Bushmen of the Kalahari Desert in Namibia and Botswana create regional social security systems that are critical to survival in harsh times. Reciprocal long-term patterns of giving and receiving gifts among the !Kung are based on their understanding that, when severe drought in one part of the Kalahari dangerously depletes food stocks, they can call on Bushmen in other parts of the Kalahari for the assistance they need to survive. Wiessner surveys research suggesting that systems of sharing within local groups of non-human primates likely have existed for millions of years and are one of the key adaptations that allowed modern humans to expand out of Africa and inhabit so many different niches on our planet. Wiessner also surveys research about hundreds of economic games conducted by economists and anthropologists in many different cultures which refute the assumption of neo-classical economics that humans only seek to maximize economic gain. This research indicates that people who care about other people have:

- a sense of fairness;
- a devotion to reciprocity;
- an aversion to inequity and inequality; and
- a taste for punishment of inequity and inequality.

A former student, Heather, described using patterns of positive and negative reciprocity in the modern American workplace. One summer she was a temporary receptionist in a vacation-time-share sales office. She worked with two salesmen she called Mr. Nice and Mr. Not–Nice who competed

---

[7]   Polly Wiessner, *Banking Time and Banking Relationships: Perspectives from Anthropology, Ethnology, and Neuroscience*, presented to the Time Banking Congress (Toronto, August 2004).

with each other to see who made the most sales. Every day, Mr. Nice and Mr. Not–Nice waited in the office lobby for couples to show up for their sales appointments. Mr. Nice talked to Heather while he waited, asking about her family and how she was doing in school. He explained to Heather how important it was for him to build relationships with his clients during his sales presentations and how he tried to be genuine with them. By contrast, Mr. Not–Nice used crude language and bragged to Heather how he deceived people in his sales presentations to make them buy time-shares they didn't really need. Because Heather pre-interviewed prospective couples before they met with a salesman, she knew which couples were nice and which were not nice. Although she was supposed to assign the first prospects of the day to the salesman who had closed the most sales the day before, she in fact assigned the nice couples to Mr. Nice and the not-nice couples to Mr. Not–Nice. Mr. Nice therefore made sales presentations to nice couples handpicked by Heather, whereas Mr. Not–Nice got all the rude and difficult couples to work with. Mr. Nice became even nicer as he closed more sales, whereas Mr. Not–Nice got angrier and ruder as his sales lagged behind.

4.   RECIPROCITY IN NEGOTIATION AND MEDIATION COMMUNICATION

As a universal principle of human behavior, reciprocity, for good or ill, is part of the dynamics of every relationship, every conversation and, therefore, every negotiation and mediation. We can ignore the operation of reciprocity in negotiation and mediation to our detriment, or we can use it effectively for our benefit.

For example, people have procedural fairness and comprehension needs. They want not just to obtain an objectively fair outcome in negotiation and mediation, but they also what to feel they have been treated fairly and were understood by the other negotiator (and the mediator).[8] Five criteria are involved in the provision and perception of procedural fairness and comprehension:

- The negotiator (or mediator) enables the other party to have an opportunity to be heard ("**voice**").
- The negotiator (or mediator) treats the other party with civility and respect ("**respect**").
- The negotiator (or mediator) consistently acts in a trustworthy way ("**trust**").
- The negotiator (or mediator) acts in a transparent, easily understood manner ("**transparency**").

---

[8]   See generally Rebecca Hollander–Blumoff, *Just Negotiation*, 88 WASH. U. L. REV. 381 (2010); and Teresa Giovaninni, *Philosophy Can Help Tribunals Draft Awards that Parties Will Accept as Legitimate*, DISPUTE RES. J. 78 (May–July 2011).

- The negotiator (or mediator) conveys objective, subjective, and holistic understanding of the other party and that party's situation ("**comprehension**").

The interjection of voice, respect, trust, transparency, and comprehension into negotiation and mediation is accomplished through use of communication and interpersonal skills, compliance with institutional norms and substantive precedent, and procedural fairness and consistency. A negotiation or mediation that incorporates voice, respect, trust, transparency, and comprehension is perceived as having "legitimacy" which creates a higher degree of satisfaction with the process. The parties' perception of legitimacy increases the likelihood they will accept and comply with the substantive outcome of the negotiation or mediation.

Positive reciprocity is at work in the "attending behaviors" of effective communication, which include maintaining eye contact and positive body posture (such as sitting up straight and leaning forward to express interest), and smiling and nodding. Other communication behaviors that can positively affect the negotiators' relationship include: showing courtesy and respect, doing the other party a favor, immediately returning a favor, making a quick concession, giving the other party needed time or information, ensuring that the other party is not caught by surprise, enabling the other party to save face, etc.

Positive reciprocity includes something as simple and commonplace in conversation as taking turns. We all have the experience of someone "hogging" a conversation and not letting us have our turn, or "butting in" and interrupting us when it is our turn to speak. We typically get frustrated (if not angry) when this happens and often we either respond in kind or withdraw from the conversation entirely, which can end the negotiation or mediation. Similarly, the principle of positive reciprocity is seen at work in the basic turn-taking protocol of negotiation and mediation (whether as taking turns listening and talking, or taking turns making offers and receiving counteroffers).

The principle of reciprocity also helps explain and predict the kind and quality of communication that occurs in negotiation and mediation. Communication in positional bargaining and distributive negotiation tends to be adversarial, competitive, and negatively reciprocal. Communication in integrative negotiation tends to be more collaborative, cooperative, and positively reciprocal. To engage in the mutual problem-solving of integrative negotiation, the parties must minimize their interpersonal conflict so they can communicate more effectively and thereby increase their willingness to work together.

A negotiator's personal communication style also can promote positive reciprocity. For example, collaborative negotiators move toward their opponents by listening to each other, establishing common ground, sharing information, emphasizing shared values, and taking individual responsibility for mutual problem-solving. Collaborative negotiators try to communicate in trustworthy, fair, objective and reasonable ways, seeking mutual gain so that both negotiators feel they have won.[9] Similarly, perspective-taking is part of the effective communication that enhances positive reciprocity. Fisher, Ury, and Patton emphasize that, "The ability to see the situation as the other side sees it, as difficult as it may be, is one of the most important skills a negotiator can possess. It is not enough to know that they see things differently. If you want to influence them, you also need to understand empathetically the power of their point of view and to feel the emotional force with which they believe in it."[10]

5. A STUDY OF RECIPROCITY IN RELATIONAL COMMUNICATION IN NEGOTIATION

Professor Forrest Russell Wood has used relational communication theory to analyze communication patterns between lawyers negotiating a simulated contract situation.[11] Relational communication is a theory of how control of a relationship is expressed by speakers during speech turns in a conversation. When speakers talk to one another, they convey messages that contain both content (e.g., information and affect) and relational instructions (which demand control, relinquish control, or share control of the relationship). The speakers generally are not aware of the relational instructions in their messages. Relational communication experts can code the messages in the speech turns in a transcript of a conversation to make the relational instructions visible:

- A message that has a relational instruction that demands that the listener respond in the next speech turn by accepting the message is called a "one-up" message, which can be coded with the symbol ↑. Such a message demands control of the relationship in the conversation. High-conflict conversations contain speech turn patterns of mostly one-up messages (↑↑↑↑) that demand control by both speakers. Demands, accusations, and allegations and denials of blame are examples of one-up messages. Wood's research showed that the less successful lawyer negotiators (i.e., those who reached fewer agreements and economically worse outcomes) used twice as many one-up messages (↑), spent more time in conflict speech turns (↑↑↑↑), did much less leveling (see below), and asked fewer questions.

---

[9] Kenneth Cloke & Joan Goldsmith, RESOLVING CONFLICTS AT WORK 213–14 (San Francisco: Jossey–Bass Publishers, 2000).

[10] Roger Fisher, William Ury, & Bruce Patton, GETTING TO YES: NEGOTIATING AGREEMENT WITHOUT GIVING IN 23 (2nd ed.) (New York: Penguin Books, 1991).

[11] Forrest Russell Wood, RELATIONAL COMMUNICATION IN NEGOTIATION INTERACTION (University of Utah: Department of Communication, December 2008).

- A response that accepts the first speaker's demand in the prior speech turn is called a "one-down" message, which can be coded with the symbol ↓. Such a message relinquishes control of the relationship in the conversation. Responses such as "You're right" and "I agree" are examples of one-down messages that relinquish control. Collaborative conversations contain speech turn patterns of alternating one-up and one-down messages (↑↓↑↓) that demand and relinquish control by both speakers.

- A response that is both non-accepting and non-demanding in relation to the prior speech turn is called a "one-across" message, which can be coded with the symbol →. Such a message shares control of the relationship in the conversation. Leveling conversations that share control contain speech turn patterns of one-across and one-down messages (→↓→↓) by both speakers. Responses such as "right," "OK," and "Uh-huh" are examples of one-across messages that have a leveling relational effect in a conversation. Asking questions that sincerely seek clarification or information also have a leveling relational effect. Wood's research showed that the more successful lawyer negotiators (i.e., those who reached more agreements and economically better outcomes) used fewer one-up messages, used more one-across and one-down messages, responded to conflict messages with more one-across and one-down messages, and asked more questions.

For his research, Wood recruited 48 lawyers and assigned them in 24 pairs to negotiate a hypothetical contract between Calomite Stables (which on very short notice needs an experienced jockey to ride its racehorse in the Kentucky Derby) and Cristo Lines (a young and upcoming jockey who is available but has never ridden before in the Derby).[12] In each pair, one lawyer represented Calomite Stables and the other lawyer represented the jockey. The lawyers were told to reach an agreement if they could. Wood video-recorded the 24 negotiations, transcribed the videos, and had the communication speech turns in each negotiation transcript coded by relational communication researchers using the relation-control coding system described above. He also had observers view the videos and indicate their responses to the ever-changing degree of closeness between the negotiators using a continuous-response measurement system (i.e., a hand-held dial). The 24 negotiations resulted in some outcomes which did not reach agreement ("the None group"), some which resulted in contracts involving only money ("the Dollar group"), and some which resulted in contracts involving both money and additional interests between the stable and the jockey ("the Dollar Plus group").

---

[12] "Negotiation in the Practice of Law: A Video Companion" (Philadelphia: American Law Institute–American Bar Association).

Wood's analysis revealed that the speech turn patterns between the negotiators had relational consequences associated with the three different negotiation outcomes. In the None group, the occurrence of competitive one-up messages (↑) and the number of reciprocal competitive speech turns of two one-up messages (↑↑) was higher. By contrast, there was a higher frequency of relational-leveling one-across messages (→) and reciprocal collaborative speech turns of two one-across messages (→→) between the negotiators in the Dollar and Dollar Plus groups. Although all of the negotiators were of similar personal and professional backgrounds, equal in power, motivated by the same issues implicit in the hypothetical negotiation, and free to combine economic and non-economic issues at will, the negotiators in the Dollar Plus group used significantly more messages, spent significantly more time interacting, addressed significantly more content issues, and agreed on significantly more content issues than did the negotiators in the None group.

Research observers of the 24 negotiation videos used real-time, continuous-response, computer-systems technology to measure the degree of "intimacy" between the negotiators by indicating on hand-held dials the amount of connectedness versus un-connectedness they perceived between the negotiators. Wood's analysis showed that, when a content offer was proposed and accepted, the mean intimacy line went up. When a period of agreement occurred during the discussion of an issue, the mean intimacy line went up. If a period of relative conflict occurred, the mean intimacy line went down. Wood's analysis also showed positive correlations between the relational coding of the negotiators' reciprocal competitive speech turns versus their reciprocal collaborative speech turns when compared to the continuous-response measurement of the degree of the perceived connectedness versus un-connectedness in their interpersonal behaviors. The more collaboratively they communicated, the more connected the observers perceived them to be. The more competitively they communicated, the more un-connected the observers perceived them to be.

Wood concludes with communication suggestions for negotiators. Before negotiating, in addition to thorough preparation (e.g., setting outcome goals, gathering information, identifying issues and interests, and assessing possible tradeoffs), Wood suggests that negotiators consider the relational consequences of how they are going to communicate with the other negotiator. By their communication choices to use more leveling messages, negotiators can co-create reciprocal collaborative speech turns and more connected interpersonal interactions, which produce more successful substantive outcomes containing more negotiated content. Therefore, during a negotiation, in addition to establishing rapport and listening for the other negotiator's perspective on core content issues, a negotiator also should focus attention on the choice of messages and avoid traditional one-up dominated messages in favor of more one-across leveling messages. Wood recommends asking questions non-aggressively as a way to create one-across leveling movements in negotiation, including asking questions about negotiation content in a one-across manner, which tends to create more cooperation. By focusing as much sensitivity on relational issues as content issues in communication, Wood believes negotiated agreements may be completed more efficiently and comprehensively, with more relational satisfaction.

6. RECIPROCITY IN REFRAMING IN NEGOTIATION AND MEDIATION

Framing and reframing are two more examples of the operation of reciprocity in negotiation and mediation communication. The tone, style, method, and substance of preparing and giving opening lines in framing a negotiation (or mediation) are critical in shaping the other negotiator's reaction. Your ability to frame the issues in a negotiation (or mediation) in a positive and motivating way can influence the other negotiator's positive reaction.

Reframing in negotiation and mediation can include looking for an unstated demand, request, or interest hiding behind a negative accusation:

Accusation: "You are selfish and care only about your work."

Demand: "Spend more time at home!"

Request: "Let's have a date night once a week."

Interest: "I want you to spend more time with me."

Suggestions about how to reframe accusations and demands into requests and interests are discussed in Chapter Three.

An unintended word choice that is perceived as a slight, criticism, or insult also can provoke a negatively reciprocal response in negotiation and mediation. For example, in a dispute in which one of the authors served as the mediator, one party (who was trying not to be confrontational) inadvertently said, "Your theory is *naive,*" when in fact he meant to say, "Your theory is *novel.*" The other party understandably took the comment as a demeaning criticism and responded in kind, which had the effect of polarizing the parties' relationship and making them less willing to work together to resolve their mutual problem.

When one negotiator makes a comment that might be intentionally negative, the other negotiator has a choice of several different kinds of responses:

• She can respond in kind, which tends to provoke an even more aggressive counter-response.

- She can reframe the remark and share it with the other party (e.g., "It sounds like you are really upset with me about what happened. Is that right?").
- She can ask for clarification and additional information (e.g., "Help me understand what you mean when you say my theory is *naive*").
- She can ignore the apparently offensive remark and respond positively, acting as though the negative remark were never uttered (e.g., "Let's talk about what we can do together now to resolve our problem.")

7. USING RECIPROCITY TO BUILD TRUST IN NEGOTIATION AND MEDIATION

Reciprocity is the tendency of others to respond in kind to how you treat them. Trust is encouraged if you treat the other person in a consistently positive, predictably trustworthy way. Trust is incentivized when you value the relationship with the other person. Trust is incentivized by your commitment to cooperative problem-solving and collaboration to resolve mutual problems. Trust is incentivized if you reward the other person for acting in a trustworthy way. Trustworthy behavior also is incentivized if the other person fears or experiences punishment for acting in an untrustworthy way.

Reciprocity-based trust is made operational when:

- You develop and maintain a reputation for acting in a trustworthy way.
- You act in a clear, consistent, predictable, respectful way.
- You tell the truth, i.e., your statements are honest and accurate.
- You keep your word, i.e., you keep your promises and fulfill your commitments.
- You reward trustworthy behavior and punish untrustworthy behavior.
- You are willing to act in a trusting way until you are betrayed by untrustworthy behavior.
- You again commit to act in a trusting way if the other person acts in a trustworthy way.

8. RECIPROCITY IN THE FOUR NEGOTIATION STRATEGIES

Reciprocity in negotiation and mediation is typically reactive: a negotiator tends to respond in kind and degree to how the other negotiator first treats him. However, reciprocity can be used proactively in negotiation and mediation: negotiators can treat others first in the manner they want the other negotiators to react, thereby influencing the likelihood other negotiators will respond in kind and degree to how they were first treated.

a. Reciprocity in Performative Negotiation

When people are treated unfairly, their sense of injustice—acting through negative reactive reciprocity—evokes anger, indignation, sometimes hatred, and occasionally even a desire for revenge, which can drive them to retaliate to inflict harm in return for perceived harm. This kind of negative reactive reciprocity tends to occur in performative negotiation (or mediation) when one negotiator first engages in condescending, posturing, bluffing, threatening, extremely aggressive, manipulative, or deceptive behaviors. These negative proactive behaviors often provoke a negative reactive response in which the second negotiator takes retaliatory action. These retaliatory behaviors can create a reciprocal escalating cycle of harm and counter-harm, revenge and counter-revenge, which eventually grows out of proportion to the initial actual or perceived harm that prompted the desire for retaliation in the first place. Such a cycle of negative reciprocity can create a "death spiral" which can destroy both the negotiation and the parties' willingness to ever work together again.

Negative reciprocity also is seen in positional bargaining (which we believe is a type of performative negotiation). In positional bargaining, each party often attempts to: confuse the other with misleading, incomplete, or inaccurate information; manipulate their relationship to get an unwarranted commitment or concession; or attempt to intimidate the other party with bluffs or threats. These negative behaviors often provoke a negative reciprocal response. Similarly, a negotiator's bargaining style also can provoke negative reciprocity. Aggressive negotiators, for example, move against their opponents, make extreme demands, give few (small and grudging) concessions, and use manipulative tactics to seek to gain unilateral advantage. This aggressive bargaining style generates distrust and misunderstanding, which often cause failures to reach agreement. Even when agreements are reached despite the adverse effects of negative reciprocity, the agreements take longer to achieve, consume more transactional costs, are not as durable, and create a greater likelihood of future retaliation.

b. Reciprocity in Transformative Negotiation

If we treat other negotiators kindly, they are more likely to react positively than if we first treat them discourteously. Positive reciprocity can range in transformative negotiation (or mediation) from extending simple courtesies to the other party (e.g., with a gratuitous tangible "gift" of water or coffee at the beginning of a negotiation or mediation session) to allowing the other party to "save face" at the end of a contentious negotiation. To give an unexpected and unrequested apology also is an attempt to use proactive positive reciprocity, which says in effect, "I hope my apology will mitigate your anger, which may help you listen to me."

c.   Reciprocity in Integrative Negotiation

Problem-solving or integrative negotiation and mediation may be regarded as a tit-for-tat game that involves a mix of cooperation (positive reciprocity) and competition (negative reciprocity). Generally, in integrative negotiation the parties cooperatively seek to expand the size of the negotiation pie before they begin to competitively allocate the amount of pie each party gets. Positive reciprocity dynamics do not just affect the attitudes and interpersonal communication of integrative negotiators; they also affect all of the Seven Elements of negotiation by:

1. increasing the negotiators' **commitment** to the problem-solving process;
2. improving their **relationship** and thereby their willingness to work together toward a mutually acceptable agreement;
3. enhancing the extent and quality of their **communication**;
4. facilitating their exchange of relevant information about their **interests** and priorities;
5. motivating their willingness to engage in generating **options**;
6. encouraging their disclosure of and willingness to consider using objective standards of **legitimacy**; and
7. disclosing and using their **alternatives** when necessary.

d.   Reciprocity in Distributive Negotiation

In distributive negotiation and mediation, each party assumes that resources are fixed and limited; therefore, each party attempts to claim resources for himself at the expense of the other. The competitive reciprocal dynamic of distributive negotiation typically plays out in a kind of zero-sum game, i.e., how much more money must one party agree to pay to the other *and* how much less money must the other party agree to accept, in order for them to reach agreement. The negative reciprocity of zero-sum competition can undermine the effectiveness, efficiency, and perceived fairness of distributive negotiation. However, if I choose to be positively proactive in distributive negotiation, I am in control of myself. If I am reactive, the other party is—to some extent—controlling my behavior. I also can be proactive in choosing not to react in kind to the other party's negative behavior, i.e., I can choose to "turn the other cheek" or "pocket the insult," which is a positive reactive intervention by which I attempt to change the otherwise negative reciprocal tit-for-tat dynamics of the ongoing negotiation.

9. A COUNTER–INTUITIVE CONCLUSION ABOUT USING POSITIVE PROACTIVE RECIPROCITY

For good or ill, reciprocity is the rocket fuel of negotiation and mediation. Positive proactive reciprocity is the golden rule of negotiation and mediation, which is under-appreciated and therefore often underutilized. One of our colleagues, who was a high school rodeo queen years ago, is now a Buddhist-trained mediator. When asked what she had learned about training horses that also applies to conducting mediations, she replied, "Always be kind."

By our choices to use more collaborative communication and more collaborative non-verbal behavior, we as negotiators and mediators can co-create reciprocal positive interpersonal interactions, which produce more fair processes and more successful substantive outcomes containing more negotiated content.

EXERCISE

Reciprocity is usually reactive, but can be used proactively. Reciprocity can be positive, i.e., paying back one good deed with another. It also can be negative, i.e., paying back one bad deed with another.

Recall some personal experience or observation of reciprocity in action in a negotiation or in a conflict—either proactive or reactive, positive or negative—and analyze how reciprocity affected the parties' relationship, their communication, and the outcome.

CHAPTER 6

THE UNIFORM MEDIATION ACT, THE MODEL STANDARDS OF CONDUCT, MEDIATION ETHICS, AND MEDIATOR CREDENTIALING AND COMPETENCY

■ ■ ■

There are thousands of state and federal statutes that deal with mediation in some form, and hundreds of laws and rules that deal with mediation privilege and confidentiality. Because it is impossible to survey all these laws and rules in a single book, this chapter that deals with mediation ethics focuses on the Uniform Mediation Act ("UMA")[1] drafted by the National Conference of Commissioners on Uniform State Laws ("NCCUSL") and on the Model Standards of Conduct for Mediators promulgated by the American Arbitration Association, the American Bar Association, and the Association for Conflict Resolution. The chapter also discusses the issues of mediator credentialing and mediator competency, which are subjects of ongoing analysis, discussion, and debate.

1. THE UNIFORM MEDIATION ACT

The NCCUSL drafted the UMA in 2001 and amended it in 2003. The District of Columbia, Idaho, Illinois, Iowa, Nebraska, New Jersey, Ohio, South Dakota, Utah, Vermont, and Washington have enacted the UMA, and it was introduced as legislation in Massachusetts and New York in 2012.

The UMA applies to legislatively-mandated, court-annexed, and privately-conducted mediation. It applies to mediation in which the parties and the mediator agree to mediate in a written record that demonstrates their expectation that mediation communications will be privileged against disclosure. It also applies to mediation conducted by a person who holds himself or herself out as a mediator. The UMA does not apply to mediations involving collective bargaining, minors in a primary or secondary school peer review process, prison inmate mediations, and some proceedings conducted by judicial officers, such as judicial settlement conferences. Similarly, unless the participants choose to invoke the UMA, the UMA does not apply to traditional cultural and

---

[1]   http://uniformlaws.org/Act.aspx?title=Mediation%20Act

religious practices that seek to resolve conflicts, solve problems, or restore relationships. These practices include Native American circle ceremonies, family conferencing, and pastoral or marital counseling.

The UMA's primary purpose is to keep mediation communications confidential. It does this by creating an evidentiary privilege so that a mediation communication is not subject to discovery or admission into evidence in a formal proceeding such as litigation or arbitration. This privilege regime is the primary means by which other kinds of communications are protected elsewhere in the law, including communications in attorney-client, doctor-patient, and priest-penitent relationships. As with these other privileges, the mediation privilege allows a person to refuse to disclose and to prevent others from disclosing mediation communications. Parties, mediators, and nonparty participants in mediation are all holders of the mediation privilege.

The UMA defines "mediation communications" as statements that are made orally, through conduct, or in writing or other recorded activity. This definition is similar to the Uniform Rule of Evidence 801, which defines a "statement" as "an oral or written assertion or nonverbal conduct of an individual who intends it as an assertion." The UMA also protects pre-mediation conversations and other communications made outside mediation sessions as "mediation communications." Promoting party candor during these initial conversations helps insure a customized, comprehensive agreement to mediate.

Written agreements to mediate and written mediated settlement agreements are not protected "mediation communications" (although parties can agree that a settlement document is confidential and will not be filed in court or otherwise made public). Mediation memoranda and other documents that are prepared by the parties for the mediator are mediation communications. Similarly, documents prepared for the mediation by experts attending the mediation would also be mediation communications. However, a tax return brought to a divorce mediation would not be a mediation communication because it was not made as part of the mediation, even though it may be used extensively in the mediation. By contrast, a note written on the tax return by a party to clarify a point for the mediator would be a mediation communication.

The NCCUSL modeled the evidentiary privilege in the UMA after the attorney-client privilege that is supported by well-developed case law. The NCCUSL expect courts to analogize the mediation privilege to the attorney-client privilege and its body of law.

There are a few exceptions to the evidentiary privilege in the UMA:

- The privilege does not apply to the underlying facts of the dispute being mediated.

- The privilege does not apply to mediations that are conducted in public.
- A person who uses mediation to plan or attempt to commit or conceal a crime cannot assert or enforce the privilege.
- The privilege does not apply to a threat to inflict bodily injury.
- The privilege does not apply to child or elderly or disabled adult abuse, neglect, abandonment, or exploitation, if the State has protected them by statute and has created an agency enforcement process.
- The privilege does not apply to proving or defending a claim of professional misconduct filed against a mediator.
- The privilege does not apply to a felony proceeding in which needed information outweighs the interest in confidentiality.
- The privilege does not apply in proceedings to enforce or nullify a mediated settlement agreement.
- Parties also may opt out of the confidentiality and privilege provisions of the UMA.

The NCCUSL believes that the UMA promotes greater certainty about mediation, because legal rules dealing with mediation are found in more than 2,500 state and federal statutes, with more than 250 statutes dealing with mediation confidentiality and privilege. This complexity creates uncertainty which the NCCUSL believes inhibits the use of mediation. The UMA also promotes greater certainty about mediation by creating a comprehensive privilege regime protecting mediation communications from disclosure. Although the UMA does not prescribe qualifications or other professional standards for mediators, the UMA does require mediators to disclose conflicts of interest before acting as a mediator and to disclose the mediator's qualifications to serve as a mediator to any party requesting that information. The NCCUSL also believes that the UMA promotes uniformity of mediation law that promotes greater understanding of mediation across state lines.

The NCCUSL believes that the protection of mediation communications from disclosure maintains the parties' and mediators' reasonable expectations about mediation confidentiality. Such confidentiality promotes the candid and informal exchange of relevant information during mediation, which enables the parties and the mediator to think constructively and creatively about ways in which the parties' differences might be resolved. A frank exchange of information is encouraged if the parties know that what is said in the mediation will not be used to their detriment in later legal proceedings.

It should be noted that an evidentiary privilege protecting mediation communications is narrower than absolute confidentiality in mediation. It is possible for mediation communications to be disclosed outside of legal proceedings, e.g., to family members, friends, business associates, and the public. If acts and statements in mediation are confidential, they cannot be voluntarily disclosed to anyone, anywhere, at any time. This is broader than the UMA's evidentiary privilege that makes mediation communications inadmissible as evidence in a subsequent legal proceeding. Therefore, Section 8 of the UMA enables parties and states to broaden confidentiality protection in mediation. Section 8 expressly provides that mediation communications are confidential "to the extent agreed by the parties or provided by other law or rule of this State."

Mediation confidentiality is regarded by many parties and by most mediators as the cornerstone of mediation. For them, the confidentiality of mediation communications against disclosure outside the mediation room is even more important to the integrity of the mediation process than the UMA mediation privilege's protection of mediation communications from disclosure in subsequent legal proceedings. In order to avail themselves of the UMA's safe harbor of confidentiality in Section 8, the parties and the mediator can agree that acts and statements in mediation are confidential. This agreement can be memorialized in a written agreement to mediate signed by the parties and by all non-party participants in the mediation. The parties, mediator, and non-party participants can expect court enforcement of this contractual agreement to keep communications in mediation confidential.

In order to maintain the parties' expectations about confidentiality, the mediator also can explain to the parties the exceptions in the UMA that require disclosure of some mediation communications. For example, in divorce mediation, the privilege does not apply to a spouse's threat (e.g., disclosed to the mediator in caucus) to inflict bodily injury on the other spouse. The mediator can disclose this threat to the other spouse. In child visitation mediation, the privilege does not apply to mediation communications about child abuse, neglect, or abandonment. In guardianship mediation, the privilege does not apply to mediation communications about elderly adult abuse or exploitation.

If the mediator intends to disclose other kinds of mediation communications, the mediator should explain that to the parties before the mediation begins. For example, some mediators in divorce mediation will not protect mediation communications about marital assets being secreted by one spouse from the other spouse. Such a waiver of the mediation privilege is effective if it is expressly waived by all parties to the mediation, orally or in a written agreement. Best practice is to have such a privilege waiver contained in the parties' written agreement to mediate.

A mediator may have additional affirmative duties of disclosure required by the mediator's professional licensing authority. For example, Model

Rule of Professional Conduct 2.4 applies to lawyers serving as mediators. A lawyer-mediator is required by Rule 2.4 to inform unrepresented parties that the lawyer is not representing them. When the lawyer-mediator knows that a party does not understand the role of a lawyer in mediation, the lawyer-mediator shall explain the difference between the lawyer's role as a third-party neutral and a lawyer's role as one who represents a client. Model Rule of Professional Conduct 8.3 also requires lawyer-mediators to report professional misconduct to the appropriate professional authority when the lawyer-mediator knows that another lawyer representing a party in mediation has committed a violation of the Rules of Professional Conduct that raises a substantial question as to that lawyer's honesty, trustworthiness, or fitness as a lawyer in other respects.

Mediation is a consensual process of self-determination in which the parties decide the resolution of their dispute themselves with the help of the mediator, rather than having the mediator impose a resolution upon them (as happens in litigation and arbitration). Parties can agree with the mediator on a specific approach to their mediation, including whether the mediator will be facilitative, evaluative, or even directive. The parties' self-determined participation in mediation allows them to create agreements that incorporate their interests and needs, which leads to greater satisfaction in both the mediation process and the substantive outcome.

A party may participate in mediation in person, by phone, electronically, or through a designated agent. Section 9(a) of the UMA allows parties to have counsel or other support persons present during mediation sessions.

Section 9 of the UMA promotes the integrity of the mediation process by requiring mediators to disclose conflicts of interest. The prospective mediator must make a reasonable inquiry to determine whether there are, and must disclose to the parties, any known facts that are likely to affect the impartiality of the mediator, including a financial or personal interest in the outcome of the mediation, and an existing or past relationship with a mediation party or foreseeable participant in the mediation (e.g., a party's counsel). Although the UMA does not require mediators to have any special qualification by background or profession, it does require mediators to be candid about their qualifications when asked. In some mediations, the parties may want to engage a mediator who has subject matter expertise in the nature of their dispute, or who has substantial experience mediating such disputes; or they may want to know whether the mediator is sufficiently competent and willing to use an evaluative or directive approach in their mediation. Although the UMA does not require these mediator disclosures about conflicts and qualifications to be made in writing, best practice is to make them in writing, with a record kept that they were provided to the parties.

Under the principle of self-determination, parties in many mediations are willing to waive a prospective mediator's disclosed conflicts of interest, e.g., the mediator may be chosen because the lawyers for the parties know the mediator and have used him as a mediator in the past. The fact that the mediator is familiar to both parties or their counsel may best qualify the mediator to mediate their dispute. That choice, however, belongs to the parties to exercise after the mediator discloses the relevant facts. This provision of the UMA solves the "repeat player" problem that arises where a mediator conducts mediations often for a particular party (e.g., a collection agency), but that fact is not disclosed to a new party.

Legislatures, courts, and parties all are interested in having disputes resolved earlier, less expensively, and with greater participant satisfaction. For example, earlier mediated settlements can promote the best interests of children affected by divorce, which means that successfully mediated divorces will not have to be tried in court, which means the legislature does not have to bear more fiscal responsibility for building new courtrooms and funding salaries for more judges.

In 2002 the United Nations Commission on International Trade Law ("UNCITRAL") adopted the Model Law on International Commercial Conciliation ("Model Law"). Section 11 of the UMA provides that international commercial mediation is governed by the UNCITRAL Model Law, unless the parties agree otherwise in writing. This provision allows parties to international commercial mediation to take advantage of the privilege protections of the UMA, which are broader than the evidentiary exclusions of the UNCITRAL Model Law.

2.   THE MODEL STANDARDS OF CONDUCT FOR MEDIATORS

The Model Standards of Conduct for Mediators ("Standards of Conduct") were most recently promulgated in 2005 by the American Arbitration Association, the American Bar Association, and the Association for Conflict Resolution. The Standards of Conduct are guidelines that contain useful advice for mediator best practice.

a.   Standard I. Self–Determination

Standard I emphasizes the principle of party self-determination in mediation. Parties have the right to come to a voluntary, un-coerced decision and make free and informed choices about the mediation process and the substantive outcome of mediation. Parties may exercise their right of self-determination at any stage of a mediation, including:

- selecting the mediator;
- designing the mediation process (subject to the mediator's duty to conduct a quality process);

- participating in or withdrawing from the mediation; and
- reaching a mediated agreement.

In trying to assure that a party is making free and informed choices in mediation, the mediator should make the parties aware of the importance of consulting other professionals to help them.

A mediator must not undermine the principle of party self-determination for any reason, including the mediator's desire to have a high settlement rate in mediation, the desire to increase the mediator's fees, or from outside pressures.

b. Standard II. Impartiality

Standard II emphasizes that a mediator must decline to serve if the mediator cannot act in an impartial manner, which means acting without favoritism, bias, prejudice, or the appearance of partiality. The mediator cannot act with partiality or prejudice based on a mediation participant's personal characteristics, background, values and beliefs, or performance at a mediation. If at any time a mediator is unable to conduct a mediation in an impartial manner, the mediator must withdraw.

A mediator should not accept (or give) a gift, favor, loan, or any other item of value that raises a question as to the mediator's actual or perceived impartiality, except that a mediator may accept (or give) gifts having *de minimis* value to facilitate a mediation or to respect cultural norms.

c. Standard III. Conflicts of Interest

Standard III emphasizes that a mediator must avoid a conflict of interest or the appearance of a conflict of interest during and after mediation. A conflict of interest can arise from the mediator having an interest in the outcome of the mediation, or from having a relationship with any mediation participant that reasonably raises a question of the mediator's impartiality.

Similar to Section 9 of the UMA discussed above, this standard requires a mediator to make a reasonable inquiry to determine whether there are any facts that are likely to create a potential or actual conflict of interest for the mediator. The mediator must disclose these actual and potential conflicts that raise a question about the mediator's impartiality. After disclosure, the mediator may proceed with the mediation, if all parties agree. This disclosure requirement continues even after accepting a mediation. If a conflict of interest undermines the integrity of the mediation process, the mediator must withdraw.

After the mediation is concluded, a mediator must not establish another relationship with any of the participants in any matter that raises questions about the integrity of the mediation, considering such factors as the time elapsed following the mediation, the nature of the relationships established, the services offered, and whether the new relationship might create a perceived or actual conflict of interest.

d. Standard IV. Competence

Standard IV emphasizes that a mediator can mediate only when the mediator has the necessary competence to satisfy the reasonable expectations of the parties concerning the mediator's competence and qualifications, training, experience in mediation, skills, cultural understandings, and other qualities creating mediator competence.

A person who offers to serve as a mediator creates the reasonable expectation that the person is competent to mediate effectively. Therefore, a mediator should maintain and enhance the mediator's knowledge and skills related to mediation, and should agree inform parties about the mediator's training, education, experience, and approach to conducting a mediation.

If, during a mediation, the mediator determines that he or she cannot conduct the mediation competently, the mediator must discuss that with the parties and address the situation, including withdrawing or requesting appropriate assistance.

A mediator shall not conduct a mediation if the mediator is impaired by drugs, alcohol, medication, or otherwise.

e. Standard V. Confidentiality

Standard V emphasizes that a mediator must maintain the confidentiality of all information obtained by the mediator in mediation, unless otherwise agreed to by the parties or required by applicable law. The mediator should not communicate to any non-participant information about how the parties acted in the mediation. Because the parties may have different expectations regarding confidentiality, the mediator must promote understanding among the parties whether and to what extent they will maintain confidentiality of the information they obtain in the mediation. The parties may make their own rules with respect to confidentiality, or the accepted practice of an individual mediator or institution may dictate a particular set of expectations about confidentiality.

Note the significant difference in this standard as compared to the UMA's mediation privilege against disclosure of mediation communications in subsequent legal proceedings. Standard V addresses the much broader scope of mediation confidentiality.

A mediator may report, if required (e.g., to the referring court), whether parties appeared at a scheduled mediation and whether or not they reached an agreement. Note, however, that an issue can arise if a party must participate in court-referred mediation in "good faith:" should this be measured objectively—e.g., by the party's mere appearance at the mediation before withdrawing, or can this be measured subjectively—by testimony about the quality of the party's participation in the mediation, without invading reasonable expectations about protecting mediation confidentiality.

A mediator who participates in teaching, research, or evaluation of mediation must protect the anonymity of the parties and abide by their reasonable expectations regarding confidentiality.

A mediator who meets with any persons in private session during a mediation shall not convey directly or indirectly to any other person, any information that was obtained during that private session without the consent of the disclosing person. Note, however, that best practice may be for the mediator to request the party in a caucus to identify specific information which the party has disclosed to the mediator which the party does not want disclosed to the other party. This can be accomplished by the mediator asking at the end of each caucus, "Is there anything you have disclosed that you do not want me to repeat?"

f.   Standard VI. Quality of the Process

Standard VI emphasizes that a mediator must conduct a mediation in a manner that promotes diligence, timeliness, safety, presence of the appropriate participants, party participation, procedural fairness, party competency, and mutual respect among all participants. Therefore, the mediator should only accept cases when the mediator can satisfy the reasonable expectation of the parties concerning the timely conduct of the mediation.

The presence or absence of persons at a mediation depends on the agreement of the parties and the mediator.

A mediator should promote honesty and candor between and among all participants, and a mediator must not knowingly misrepresent any material fact or circumstance in the course of a mediation.

The role of a mediator differs substantially from other professional roles (e.g., a lawyer, counselor, psychologist, etc.), and mixing the role of a mediator and the role of another profession is problematic. A mediator shall not conduct a dispute resolution procedure other than mediation (e.g., early neutral evaluation or non-binding arbitration) but label it mediation in an effort to gain the protection of the law pertaining to mediation (e.g., solely to make communications confidential or privileged). However, a mediator may recommend that parties consider resolving their dispute through arbitration, counseling, neutral evaluation, or other processes. A mediator shall not undertake an additional dispute resolution role (e.g., becoming the arbitrator) in the same matter without the informed consent of the parties. A mediator who undertakes such an additional role assumes different duties and responsibilities governed by other standards, with which the mediator must comply.

A mediator may provide information to the parties that the mediator is qualified by training or experience to provide (e.g., give them an expert evaluation of their dispute), only if the mediator can do so competently.

If a mediation is being used to further criminal conduct, the mediator should withdraw from or terminate the mediation. Note that this standard does not address whether a party's expectation of confidentiality is waived, as does the UMA.

If a party appears to have difficulty comprehending the mediation process, issues, or settlement options, or has difficulty participating in the mediation, the mediator should explore the circumstances and make the necessary accommodations, modifications, or adjustments required by the principle of party self-determination.

If a mediator is made aware of domestic abuse or violence among the parties, the mediator should withdraw from or terminate the mediation. Note that this standard is inconsistent with the well-recognized practice of trained, expert mediators conducting divorce or child visitation mediations in which domestic violence is an issue. This standard also does not address issues of child or elderly or disabled adult abuse, neglect, abandonment, or exploitation, and whether they are exempt from the parties' expectation of confidentiality.

g.   Standard VII. Advertising and Solicitation

Standard VII emphasizes that a mediator must be truthful and not misleading when advertising, soliciting, or otherwise communicating the mediator's qualifications, experience, services, and fees. The mediator should not include any promises as to outcome in advertising materials (e.g., "I will settle your case"), including in business cards, stationery, or computer-based communications. A mediator should only claim to meet the mediator qualifications of a governmental entity or private organization (if that entity or organization has a recognized procedure for qualifying mediators), if it has granted that status to the mediator. Without their permission, a mediator shall not mention the names of former parties in promotional materials or through other forms of communication.

h.   Standard VIII. Fees and Other Charges

Standard VIII emphasizes that a mediator must provide each party or representative true and complete information about mediation fees, expenses, and any other actual or potential charges that may be incurred in connection with a mediation. The mediator's fees should be based on relevant factors, including the type and complexity of the matter, the qualifications of the mediator, the time required, and the customary rates for such mediation services. Best practice is that the mediator's fee arrangement with the parties should be in writing. A mediator may accept unequal fee payments from the parties, so long as this does not adversely affect the mediator's ability to conduct a mediation in an impartial manner.

i.   Standard IX. Advancement of Mediation Practice

Standard IX emphasizes that a mediator should act in a manner that advances the practice of mediation by:

- fostering diversity within the field of mediation;
- making mediation accessible to those who elect to use it, including providing services at a reduced rate or on a pro bono basis;
- participating in research, including obtaining participant feedback when appropriate;
- participating in outreach and education efforts to assist the public in developing an improved understanding of, and appreciation for, mediation;
- assisting newer mediators through training, mentoring, and networking;
- demonstrating respect for differing points of view within the mediation field;
- seeking to learn from other mediators; and
- working with other mediators to improve the profession and better serve people in conflict.

3.   MEDIATOR CREDENTIALING

In 2012, the Alternative Dispute Resolution Section ("ADR Section") of the American Bar Association's Task Force ("Task Force") on Mediator Credentialing issued its Final Report ("ABA Final Report").[2] The ABA Final Report acknowledges that the issue of mediator credentialing is an evolving and controversial topic. Although many private mediation organizations and some courts and agencies offer forms of credentialing or certification, (e.g., by establishing requirements for membership on mediator panels), there is no nationwide system of credentialing, because there are different opinions about its desirability. The Task Force reviewed whether the ADR Section should adopt a policy on this issue and concluded that "credentialing" has no precise meaning.

---

[2]   http://www.americanbar.org/content/dam/aba/images/dispute_resolution/Credentialing TaskForce.pdf

Most of the private organizations and courts which maintain mediator panels require their mediator candidates to complete an approved mediation training program. Some programs provide a certificate to those who complete the training, but do not require graduates to demonstrate specific competencies. Other organizations require their mediator candidates to demonstrate specific skills through a testing process. Some organizations require their mediators to provide client assessments which are made available to the public.

The most demanding credentialing programs require:

- completion of a training program, usually 30 to 40 hours long, which includes significant mediation role-playing;
- observation of one or more actual mediations;
- experience as a co-mediator in one or more actual mediations; and
- an assessment process in which the candidate is graded on competence skills demonstrated in a role-played dispute.

The Task Force observed, however, that the mediation community has not reached a consensus about which skills and knowledge competent mediators must possess.

Task Force members agreed that credentialing is in the public interest when an organization or court requires parties to use mediators on its panel. When this occurs, the organization or court must ensure that its mediators are competent.

The Task Force made a number of recommendations:

1. The credentialing organization should clearly define the skills, knowledge, and values which mediators that it credentials must possess. Credentials should be tailored for specific kinds of mediation requiring unique skills, knowledge, and values (e.g., divorce, family disputes involving domestic violence, victim-offender mediation, etc.).

2. The credentialing organization should ensure that mediators have training adequate to instill the requisite skills, knowledge, and values. The training should include:

   a. Substantial instruction, including experience acting as mediator in role-played disputes of the kind for which the mediator seeks credentials.

   b. Observation of one or more actual mediations.

   c. Co-mediator experience mediating one or more actual cases with a credentialed mediator.

3. To avoid a conflict of interest, the credentialing should be administered by an organization distinct from the organization, which trains the mediator.

4. The mediator assessment process should be capable of consistently and accurately determining whether mediator candidates possess the requisite skills, knowledge, and values.

5. The credentialing organization should explain clearly to parties, who are likely to rely on its credential, what is being certified.

6. The credentialing organization should provide an easily accessible process for registering complaints against its credentialed mediators. The organization should promptly and fairly investigate complaints and, if appropriate, sanction mediators (including de-credentialing) who fail to comply with the organization's standards.

7. A majority of the Task Force believed that the credentialing organization should have a feedback process for monitoring the performance of its credentialed mediators.

8. Credentialing should not exclude new methods of resolving disputes or exclude mediators with non-traditional backgrounds.

The Task Force recommended against credentialing systems that:

- operate as mandatory licensing;
- bar non-lawyers from becoming credentialed;.
- bar parties from selecting a non-credentialed mediator.

4. PERFORMANCE–BASED LEARNING OBJECTIVES FOR BASIC MEDIATION TRAINING[3]

Task 1: Conduct Pre–Mediation Conferences

Obj. 1.1: Understand the purposes of pre-mediation communications with lawyers and/or parties, including any expectations of confidentiality concerning ex parte communications.

Obj. 1.2: Inquire, identify, and disclose (in writing) potential conflicts of interest (especially existing and prior relationships with parties, lawyers, and law firms, plus any financial or personal interest in the outcome of the mediation) that may affect the appearance of impartiality.

Obj. 1.3: If asked, identify and disclose (in writing) qualifications to serve as the mediator (e.g., style and philosophy of mediation, subject matter expertise, advanced training, experience in similar mediations, whether evaluative mediation may be expected, etc.).

---

[3] A group of Utah mediators, including Professor Holbrook, identified these mediator tasks and related mediation training objectives. Together, the tasks and objectives can serve as a checklist of mediator competencies.

Obj. 1.4:   Screen for and discuss expectations, relationships, issues, situations, or circumstances that affect suitability and timing for mediation. Ask questions to determine any special considerations that should apply before, during, or after mediation. Answer questions about mediation or the mediator.

Obj. 1.5:   Discuss documents that should be provided to the mediator before the mediation, who will provide them and when, whether the parties will submit pre-mediation statements and, if so, whether they will be exchanged or submitted confidentially.

Obj. 1.6:   Discuss the mediator's written agreement to mediate, the mediator's fees and costs, allocation issues, method of payment (e.g., pre-mediation deposits or post-mediation billing statements), etc.

Obj. 1.7:   Determine the mediator's availability and schedule the date, time, location, and any special arrangements for the mediation.

Task: Convene the Mediation

Obj. 2.1:   During role-play simulations, the mediator will establish rapport by introducing him/herself to the parties, introduce all parties present, and place the parties at ease by engaging in informal, neutral talk.

Obj. 2.2:   Deliver an opening statement that includes the fundamental components governing mediation.

Obj. 2.3:   During simulations, obtain signatures on the agreement to mediate prior to beginning the negotiation.

Task: Facilitate Communication

Obj. 3.1:   Distinguish the differences among and uses of various types of questioning techniques (e.g. open, closed, and exploratory or hypothetical questions, etc.).

Obj. 3.2:   While acting as mediator during role-play scenarios, ask appropriate questions to elicit information, generate options, check reality, etc.

Obj. 3.3:   While acting as mediator during role-play scenarios, use verbal and nonverbal listening skills to convey attention and verify understanding.

Obj. 3.4:   While acting as mediator during role-play scenarios, neutralize position statements using a variety of techniques (e.g. reframing, asking clarifying questions, etc.).

Obj. 3.5:   While acting as mediator during role-play scenarios, create a written or verbal agenda of topics or issues to be covered during the mediation.

Obj. 3.6:   Distinguish among positions, issues, and interests.

Obj. 3.7:   While acting as mediator during role-play scenarios, utilize communication skills to help parties identify, express, and clarify underlying interests.

Obj. 3.8:   Self-assess the student's level of comfort in the presence of high emotion.

Obj. 3.9:   While acting as mediator during role-play scenarios, use listening skills to manage high emotion.

Obj. 3.10:   While acting as mediator during role-play scenarios, demonstrate mediator respect and impartiality.

Obj. 3.11:   Recognize personal values, beliefs, and biases that could compromise the student's impartiality as a mediator.

Obj. 3.12:   Acknowledge the parties' efforts toward progress.

Obj. 3.13:   Recognize various approaches to help motivate the parties' willingness to make additional movement.

Obj. 3.14:   Use appropriate communication techniques to help parties maintain a forward-looking focus (e.g. reframing, questioning, encouraging, validating, etc.).

Task: Facilitate Negotiation and Decision Making

Obj. 4.1:   Recognize strategies used in negotiation and identify the appropriate uses for each strategy.

Obj. 4.2:   Identify types of power that can affect parties in mediation.

Obj. 4.3:   Identify strategies for managing power imbalances during mediation.

Obj. 4.4:   Recognize process options that further the clients' goals (e.g. order of presentation, staying in joint session, use of caucus, excluding lawyers, etc.).

Obj. 4.5:   Demonstrate the ability to elicit, identify, and verify the parties' needs and wants using appropriate learning techniques.

Obj. 4.6:   While acting as mediator during role-play scenarios, summarize areas of agreement between parties to help move the mediation forward.

Obj. 4.7:   Identify the guidelines for effective brainstorming.

Obj. 4.8:   Acting as a mediator, facilitate brainstorming with the parties.

Obj. 4.9:   While acting as mediator during role-play scenarios, ask questions to help parties assess the reality and practicability of following agreement options.

Obj. 4.10:   While acting as mediator during role-play scenarios, ask questions to help parties assess the consequences of not reaching agreement during mediation.

Obj. 4.11:   While acting as mediator in role-play simulations, demonstrate different strategies for overcoming impasses (e.g. brainstorming, risk analysis, use of silence, use of hypotheticals, evaluate BATNAs, role reversal, end-game techniques, etc.).

Task: Conclude the Mediation Appropriately

Obj. 5.1:   Identify situations when mediation should be terminated.

Obj. 5.2:   List the options that clients may select for post-mediation documentation and discuss the potential outcomes of each option (e.g. draft a list of agreement terms, draft an unsigned MOU, draft a signed MOU, draft an enforceable agreement, have lawyers draft a document, have no document, etc).

Obj. 5.3:   Identify components of well-written agreements.

Obj. 5.4:   Explain the ethical considerations of writing agreements.

Obj. 5.5:   Distinguish between effective and ineffective statements in an agreement.

Obj. 5.6:   Acting as mediator, conclude the mediation by summarizing the points of agreement or impasse, elicit affirmation of the parties' concurrence with these points of agreement or impasse, ask questions to clarify the parties' commitments for next steps, and discuss methods for future communication between the parties, if appropriate.

Task: Complete Post–Mediation Tasks

Obj. 6.1:   Write a clear and concise memorandum of understanding or other appropriate document that summarizes the points of agreement derived in mediation.

Obj. 6.2:   Recognize the legal and ethical implications of creating a memorandum of understanding, who should draft the document, and the issues involved in the clients' signing the document.

Obj. 6.3:   List the types of information or documents that mediators should retain and explain the purposes for retaining this information.

Obj. 6.4:   List the types of information or documents that mediators should destroy after completing the mediation and explain the purpose for destroying this information.

Task: Communicate Information to Others

Obj. 7.1:   Recognize situations when an outside specialist could assist the parties (e.g. mental health professionals, accounting specialists, tax specialists, etc.).

Obj. 7.2:   List sources of information about legal rights and recourses that could help parties make good decisions in mediation.

Obj. 7.3:   Explain best practice guidelines when making referrals (e.g. refer to panels or lists rather than to a single individual, take no compensation for referrals, etc.).

Obj. 7.4:   Identify when it would be appropriate to provide information to lawyers and how to present this information in a balanced way.

Obj. 7.5:   Recognize that some mediation programs may require special documentation.

Task: Pursue Continual Learning and Improvement

Obj. 8.1:   Create a personal action plan to develop mediation skills beyond this workshop.

Task: Understand Mediation Concepts

Obj. 9.1:   Distinguish mediation from other forms of dispute resolution (negotiation, litigation, arbitration, judicial settlement conference, early neutral evaluation, etc.).

Obj. 9.2:   Identify causes of conflict.

Obj. 9.3:   List strengths and weakness of different conflict styles and strategies.

Obj. 9.4:   Identify the student's personal style for dealing with conflict.

Obj. 9.5:   Identify the student's cultural orientation toward conflict.

Obj. 9.6:   Identify strategies for facilitating conflicts between disputants from different cultural orientations.

Obj. 9.7:   Given sample scenarios that illustrate ethical dilemmas and legal reporting requirements for mediators, propose appropriate actions that align with the ethical practice of mediation.

Obj. 9.8: Gain familiarity with current ethical guidelines that govern the practice of mediation (the ACR Standards of Conduct for Mediators and other national standards governing mediation; and in Utah: the ADR Act, U.C.A. 78–31b–1, et seq.; Uniform Mediation Act, U.C.A. 78–31c–101, et seq.; Rule 4–510; and Utah Rules of Court–Annexed Dispute Resolution (URCADR)).

Task: Understand Mediator Abilities and Attributes

Obj. 10.1: Gain awareness of the qualities and characteristics of a skilled mediator and assess one's own strengths and areas for improvement.

APPENDIX A

UNIFORM MEDIATION ACT

■ ■ ■

(Last Revised or Amended in 2003)

Drafted by the
NATIONAL CONFERENCE OF COMMISSIONERS
ON UNIFORM STATE LAWS

Section 1. **Title.** This [Act] may be cited as the Uniform Mediation Act.

Section 2. **Definitions.** In this [Act]:

(1) "Mediation" means a process in which a mediator facilitates communication and negotiation between parties to assist them in reaching a voluntary agreement regarding their dispute.

(2) "Mediation communication" means a statement, whether oral or in a record or verbal or nonverbal, that occurs during a mediation or is made for purposes of considering, conducting, participating in, initiating, continuing, or reconvening a mediation or retaining a mediator.

(3) "Mediator" means an individual who conducts a mediation.

(4) "Nonparty participant" means a person, other than a party or mediator, that participates in a mediation.

(5) "Mediation party" means a person that participates in a mediation and whose agreement is necessary to resolve the dispute.

(6) "Person" means an individual, corporation, business trust, estate, trust, partnership, limited liability company, association, joint venture, government; governmental subdivision, agency, or instrumentality; public corporation, or any other legal or commercial entity.

(7) "Proceeding" means:

(A) a judicial, administrative, arbitral, or other adjudicative process, including related pre-hearing and post-hearing motions, conferences, and discovery; or

(B) a legislative hearing or similar process.

(8) "Record" means information that is inscribed on a tangible medium or that is stored in an electronic or other medium and is retrievable in perceivable form.

(9) "Sign" means:

(A) to execute or adopt a tangible symbol with the present intent to authenticate a record; or

(B) to attach or logically associate an electronic symbol, sound, or process to or with a record with the present intent to authenticate a record.

Section 3.   Scope.

(a) Except as otherwise provided in subsection (b) or (c), this [Act] applies to a mediation in which:

(1) the mediation parties are required to mediate by statute or court or administrative agency rule or referred to mediation by a court, administrative agency, or arbitrator;

(2) the mediation parties and the mediator agree to mediate in a record that demonstrates an expectation that mediation communications will be privileged against disclosure; or

(3) the mediation parties use as a mediator an individual who holds himself or herself out as a mediator or the mediation is provided by a person that holds itself out as providing mediation.

(b) The [Act] does not apply to a mediation:

(1) relating to the establishment, negotiation, administration, or termination of a collective bargaining relationship;

(2) relating to a dispute that is pending under or is part of the processes established by a collective bargaining agreement, except that the [Act] applies to a mediation arising out of a dispute that has been filed with an administrative agency or court;

(3) conducted by a judge who might make a ruling on the case; or

(4) conducted under the auspices of:

(A) a primary or secondary school if all the parties are students or

(B) a correctional institution for youths if all the parties are residents of that institution.

(c) If the parties agree in advance in a signed record, or a record of proceeding reflects agreement by the parties, that all or part of a mediation is not privileged, the privileges under Sections 4 through 6 do not apply to the mediation or part agreed upon. However, Sections 4 through 6 apply to a mediation communication made by a person that has not received actual notice of the agreement before the communication is made.

Section 4.   Privilege against disclosure; admissibility; discovery.

(a) Except as otherwise provided in Section 6, a mediation communication is privileged as provided in subsection (b) and is not subject to discovery or admissible in evidence in a proceeding unless waived or precluded as provided by Section 5.

(b) In a proceeding, the following privileges apply:

(1) A mediation party may refuse to disclose, and may prevent any other person from disclosing, a mediation communication.

(2) A mediator may refuse to disclose a mediation communication, and may prevent any other person from disclosing a mediation communication of the mediator.

(3) A nonparty participant may refuse to disclose, and may prevent any other person from disclosing, a mediation communication of the nonparty participant.

(c) Evidence or information that is otherwise admissible or subject to discovery does not become inadmissible or protected from discovery solely by reason of its disclosure or use in a mediation.

Section 5.   Waiver and preclusion of privilege.

(a) A privilege under Section 4 may be waived in a record or orally during a proceeding if it is expressly waived by all parties to the mediation and:

(1) in the case of the privilege of a mediator, it is expressly waived by the mediator; and

(2) in the case of the privilege of a nonparty participant, it is expressly waived by the nonparty participant.

(b) A person that discloses or makes a representation about a mediation communication which prejudices another person in a proceeding is precluded from asserting a privilege under Section 4, but only to the extent necessary for the person prejudiced to respond to the representation or disclosure.

(c) A person that intentionally uses a mediation to plan, attempt to commit or commit a crime, or to conceal an ongoing crime or ongoing criminal activity is precluded from asserting a privilege under Section 4.

Section 6.   Exceptions to privilege.

(a) There is no privilege under Section 4 for a mediation communication that is:

(1) in an agreement evidenced by a record signed by all parties to the agreement;

(2) available to the public under [insert statutory reference to open records act] or made during a session of a mediation which is open, or is required by law to be open, to the public;

(3) a threat or statement of a plan to inflict bodily injury or commit a crime of violence;

(4) intentionally used to plan a crime, attempt to commit or commit a crime, or to conceal an ongoing crime or ongoing criminal activity;

(5) sought or offered to prove or disprove a claim or complaint of professional misconduct or malpractice filed against a mediator;

(6) except as otherwise provided in subsection (c), sought or offered to prove or disprove a claim or complaint of professional misconduct or malpractice filed against a mediation party, nonparty participant, or representative of a party based on conduct occurring during a mediation; or

(7) sought or offered to prove or disprove abuse, neglect, abandonment, or exploitation in a proceeding in which a child or adult protective services agency is a party, unless the

[Alternative A: [State to insert, for example, child or adult protection] case is referred by a court to mediation and a public agency participates.]

[Alternative B: public agency participates in the [State to insert, for example, child or adult protection] mediation].

(b) There is no privilege under Section 4 if a court, administrative agency, or arbitrator finds, after a hearing in camera, that the party seeking discovery or the proponent of the evidence has shown that the evidence is not otherwise available, that there is a need for the evidence that substantially outweighs the interest in protecting confidentiality, and that the mediation communication is sought or offered in:

(1) a court proceeding involving a felony [or misdemeanor]; or

(2) except as otherwise provided in subsection (c), a proceeding to prove a claim to rescind or reform or a defense to avoid liability on a contract arising out of the mediation.

(c) A mediator may not be compelled to provide evidence of a mediation communication referred to in subsection (a)(6) or (b)(2).

(d) If a mediation communication is not privileged under subsection (a) or (b), only the portion of the communication necessary for the application of the exception from nondisclosure may be admitted. Admission of evidence under subsection (a) or (b) does not render the evidence, or any other mediation communication, discoverable or admissible for any other purpose.

Section 7. Prohibited mediator reports.

(a) Except as required in subsection (b), a mediator may not make a report, assessment, evaluation, recommendation, finding, or other communication regarding a mediation to a court, administrative agency, or other authority that may make a ruling on the dispute that is the subject of the mediation.

(b) A mediator may disclose:

(1) whether the mediation occurred or has terminated, whether a settlement was reached, and attendance;

(2) a mediation communication as permitted under Section 6; or

(3) a mediation communication evidencing abuse, neglect, abandonment, or exploitation of an individual to a public agency responsible for protecting individuals against such mistreatment.

(c) A communication made in violation of subsection (a) may not be considered by a court, administrative agency, or arbitrator.

Section 8. Confidentiality.

Unless subject to the [insert statutory references to open meetings act and open records act], mediation communications are confidential to the extent agreed by the parties or provided by other law or rule of this State.

Section 9. Mediator's disclosure of conflicts of interest; background.

(a) Before accepting a mediation, an individual who is requested to serve as a mediator shall:

(1) make an inquiry that is reasonable under the circumstances to determine whether there are any known facts that a reasonable individual would consider likely to affect the impartiality of the mediator, including a financial or personal interest in the outcome of the mediation and an existing or past relationship with a mediation party or foreseeable participant in the mediation; and

(2) disclose any such known fact to the mediation parties as soon as is practical before accepting a mediation.

(b) If a mediator learns any fact described in subsection (a)(1) after accepting a mediation, the mediator shall disclose it as soon as is practicable.

(c) At the request of a mediation party, an individual who is requested to serve as a mediator shall disclose the mediator's qualifications to mediate a dispute.

(d) A person that violates subsection [(a) or (b)][(a), (b), or (g)] is precluded by the violation from asserting a privilege under Section 4.

(e) Subsections (a), (b), [and] (c), [and] [(g)] do not apply to an individual acting as a judge.

(f) This [Act] does not require that a mediator have a special qualification by background or profession.

[(g) A mediator must be impartial, unless after disclosure of the facts required in subsections (a) and (b) to be disclosed, the parties agree otherwise.]

Section 10. Participation in mediation.

An lawyer or other individual designated by a party may accompany the party to and participate in a mediation. A waiver of participation given before the mediation may be rescinded.

Section 11. International commercial media.

(a) In this section, "Model Law" means the Model Law on International Commercial Conciliation adopted by the United Nations Commission on International Trade Law on 28 June 2002 and recommended by the United Nations General Assembly in a resolution (A/RES/57/18) dated 19 November 2002, and "international commercial mediation" means an international commercial conciliation as defined in Article 1 of the Model Law.

(b) Except as otherwise provided in subsections (c) and (d), if a mediation is an international commercial mediation, the mediation is governed by the Model Law.

(c) Unless the parties agree in accordance with Section 3(c) of this [Act] that all or part of an international commercial mediation is not privileged, Sections 4, 5, and 6 and any applicable definitions in Section 2 of this [Act] also apply to the mediation and nothing in Article 10 of the Model Law derogates from Sections 4, 5, and 6.

(d) If the parties to an international commercial mediation agree under Article 1, subsection (7), of the Model Law that the Model Law does not apply, this [Act] applies.

Section 12. Relation to electronic signatures in global and national commerce act. This [Act] modifies, limits, or supersedes the federal Electronic Signatures in Global and National Commerce Act, 15 U.S.C. Section 7001 et seq., but this [Act] does not modify, limit, or supersede Section 101(c) of that Act or authorize electronic delivery of any of the notices described in Section 103(b) of that Act.

Section 13. Uniformity of application and construction.

In applying and construing this [Act], consideration should be given to the need to promote uniformity of the law with respect to its subject matter among States that enact it.

Section 14. Severability clause.

If any provision of this [Act] or its application to any person or circumstance is held invalid, the invalidity does not affect other provisions or applications of this [Act] which can be given effect without the invalid provision or application, and to this end the provisions of this [Act] are severable.

Section 15. Effective date.

This [Act] takes effect . . . .

Section 16. Repeals.

The following acts and parts of acts are hereby repealed:

Section 17. Application to existing agreements or referrals.

(a) This [Act] governs a mediation pursuant to a referral or an agreement to mediate made on or after [the effective date of this [Act]].

(b) On or after [a delayed date], this [Act] governs an agreement to mediate whenever made.

INDEX

References are to Pages